The Ten Commandments
for Everyday Life

"Fr. Max has done another beautiful job of taking ancient wisdom and timeless spiritual principles and turning them into useful application in the modern world. His approach is human and down to earth, applicable to anyone in any spiritual tradition and practice. He helps you see that the Ten Commandments are not meant to be restrictive but, in fact, are meant to give you freedom."

—David Irvine, author of *Becoming Real: Journey to Authenticity* and *The Authentic Leader: It's About Presence, Not Position*

"Having explored the virtuous life in *Beatitudes for the Workplace*, Jesuit Max Oliva now invites us to reflect on the moral life in his sequel. Scripturally referenced throughout, *The 10 Commandments for Everyday Life* is accessible, engaging and consistently insightful. It appeals to a wide audience and is an invaluable companion to Ignatius' Examen, speaking to our experience, heart and conscience, our habits of being."

—Mary Romo, Adjunct Professor of Rhetoric and Language at the University of San Francisco and parish RCIA facilitator

"Fr. Max Oliva has written a compelling contemporary exploration of the relevance of the Ten Commandments to living an ethical, faith-filled life. Full of thoughtful prayer and wisdom, this book will encourage and challenge any reader to become a better person. It simply is a winner!"

—Hank Shea, Senior Distinguished Fellow at the University of St. Thomas School of Law in Minneapolis and a University Associate at the University of Arizona Rogers College of Law in Tucson

"With gentle words and memorable stories, Fr. Oliva transforms commandments that many learned as 'restrictions' into welcoming guides to a joy-filled life. These short and memorable essays from an exceptional spiritual guide connect tradition to the challenges of contemporary circumstances."

—André L. Delbecq, J. Thomas and Kathleen McCarthy University Professor, Santa Clara University

"The personal stories and life experiences shared bring the commandments alive. Fr. Max is skilled at asking reflection questions that will challenge you to seek Christ in a personal and powerful way. If we lived out the commandments in the ways illustrated in this book, we would change society."

—Tracy Tomiak, MRE/C Marriage and Family Counsellor and author of *Thriving Not Just Surviving: Living Abundantly with Pain*

"Fr. Max Oliva's views on the Ten Commandments jump off the page and wrestle with our modern culture. The wisdom of this book reflects a man who has spent his life teaching ethics and helping souls in need. His observations are insightful and thought provoking."

—Bob Brown, President of Opportunity Village, Las Vegas, Nevada

The Ten Commandments
for Everyday Life

Max Oliva SJ

NOVALIS

Cover design: Blair Turner
Layout: Audrey Wells

Published by Novalis

Publishing Office
10 Lower Spadina Avenue, Suite 400
Toronto, Ontario, Canada
M5V 2Z2

Head Office
4475 Frontenac Street
Montréal, Québec, Canada
H2H 2S2

www.novalis.ca

Library and Archives Canada Cataloguing in Publication

Oliva, Max, 1939-, author
        The Ten commandments for everyday life / Fr. Max Oliva SJ.

Issued in print and electronic formats.

ISBN 978-2-89688-148-2 (pbk.).--ISBN 978-2-89688-149-9 (epub).--
ISBN 978-2-89688-150-5 (mobi).--ISBN 978-2-89688-151-2 (pdf)

        1. Ten commandments--Criticism, interpretation, etc. 2. Christian life--Catholic authors.
3. Christian ethics--Catholic authors. I. Title.

BV4655.O45 2015   241.5'   C2014-906836-0
                                         C2014-906837-9

Printed in Canada.

We acknowledge the financial support of the Government of Canada through the Canada Book Fund for business development activities.

5 4 3 2 1   19   18   17   16   15

Acknowledgements

First of all, I want to thank Joseph Sinasac, publisher of Novalis, for asking me to write a sequel to my book *Beatitudes for the Workplace*, which Novalis published in 2009. The idea to base the follow-up book on the Ten Commandments also came from Joseph. I write a monthly column on the Internet called "Spirituality and Ethics." After the publication of the Beatitudes book, I wrote a series on the commandments and their relevance for today. Joseph read the articles and thought they would be a good framework for another book. I agreed.

I wrote this book in Las Vegas, Nevada, where I have lived since 2011. The title of my ministry is "Ethics in the Marketplace." I am grateful to Bishop Joseph Pepe, the Bishop of the Las Vegas Diocese, for his affirmation and encouragement of this ministry and other works that I do here.

One of the first actions I took after moving to Las Vegas from San Jose, California, was to form an Advisory Committee. I needed help to understand the culture of Las Vegas. I also needed suggestions on how best to use my gifts in this part of the world. I am deeply grateful for the generosity of my advisors, who have given of their time and ideas. They are Bob Brown, Michael Buckley, Marlene Richter, Gian Brown, Mike Bonner, Jeanne Hamrick, John Laub, Joe Brown and Susan Sullivan.

Special thanks to Diane Gibes, who helped design the marketing brochure for "Ethics in the Marketplace," and to Jeff Nelson, who designed and updates my website (www.ethicsinthemarket place.com).

In addition are the following men and women who have played a significant role in developing the ideas for this book: Jim Lamb, Fred and Bernie Conte, Heather Jamieson, Dominic Marrocco, Sister Theresa McGrath, CCVI, Steve Curtis, Edward Bevilacqua Sr. and Ed Bevilacqua Jr., Sister Janet Akerman, O.P., Tom Miller, Gregor Ros, and Deacons Jacob Favela and Tim O'Callaghan.

My ministry in the Vegas valley also consists of presiding at weekday and Sunday Masses. I do this at three parishes: St. Christopher's, where I live, Christ the King, and Guardian Angel Cathedral. I am grateful to the pastors for this opportunity to serve and to their congregations for their welcoming ways.

I want to thank Fr. Ron Zanoni (former pastor) and Fr. Alberto Alzate and the staff and parishioners of St. Christopher's for their encouraging support as I wrote the book.

I belong to the Society of Jesus (Jesuits). We are community-oriented. However, I am the only Jesuit living in southern Nevada. This means my immediate community consists of people in the local area. I want to recognize the following families for their warm hospitality and for the support they give to me: Barbara J. Buckley, her son Kevin and his wife Silvia, Connie and Tom Mazelin, Bill Mazelin, Sam and Maria Romero, Bob and Melinda Brown, Chuck and Katie Gebhardt, Gail and Donna Andress, and the Barnaby family. Add to these the lively Friday lunch group that meets weekly in nearby Boulder City, where I often take my day off.

Speaking of Jesuits, they are my brothers, and without their ongoing support I could not survive out here in the desert. Special thanks to Fr. Mike Weiler, my religious superior who missioned me to ministry in Las Vegas, to Fr. John Mossi for his encouragement and brotherly support, and to the California Province Jesuit communities at the Loyola Institute, Bellarmine College Prep and Santa Clara University. To the retired Jesuit priests and brothers at the Sacred Heart Center in Los Gatos, California, I am grateful for their prayers for the desert mission.

Finally, but not least, is my editor. This is the second time I have had the privilege of working with Anne Louise Mahoney. I have learned a lot from her and especially appreciate her attention to detail.

Contents

* The chapter titles follow the traditional Catholic catechetical formula.
  In this book, the Sixth and Ninth Commandments are combined in the
  same chapter.

Introduction

....

This book is a sequel to my 2009 book, *Beatitudes for the Workplace* – the difference being that in this volume we are focusing on the Ten Commandments and their relevance today.

While my last work was all about the workplace, this one turns to both our personal and professional lives. The book is scripturally based. In addition, I draw from a variety of authors and the *Catechism of the Catholic Church*. There are personal stories, both from my own life and from the lives of others who graciously agreed to share their insights. The footnotes for each commandment provide the reader with opportunities for further reading and reflection. I combined commandments six ("You shall not commit adultery.") and nine ("You shall not covet your neighbour's wife.") because they overlap.

The commandments are divided into two parts. The first three point us in the direction of our creaturehood and our respect for the Creator; in Jesus' words, this refers to loving the Lord our God with all our heart, and all our soul, and all our mind (Luke 10:27). Numbers four to ten refer to our interpersonal relationships – how we treat one another; as Jesus says, this is loving our neighbour as ourselves (Luke 10:27).

The traditional way of reading most of the Ten Commandments is in the negative form of 'Do nots': "Do not kill, steal, covet, etc." Ian Knox, in his book *Theology for Teachers*, offers a positive rendering of each:

I.   Recognize, accept, and worship only the One, True God.
II. Respect and reverence God.
III. Remember the Sabbath day, and keep it holy.
IV. Honor your father and your mother.
V.   Respect life, and the bodily integrity of every person, including your own.
VI. Respect the integrity of married life.
VII. Respect the personal freedom of others.
VIII.Respect the truth.
IX. Respect the integrity of marriage even in intention and desire.
X.   Respect the right of your neighbor to own property.[1]

Rabbi Abraham Joshua Heschel expands in a positive way on the third commandment: "Six days a week we wrestle with the world, wringing profit from the earth; on the Sabbath we especially care for the seed of eternity planted in the soul."[2]

The Ten Commandments are concerned with basic human morality. Pope Francis writes, "they show us a path to travel and also constitute a sort of 'moral code' for building just societies that are made for men and women."[3]

Our faithful and providential God, out of love for humanity, gave us the commandments, through Moses, to help free us from whatever enslaves us. Rather than limiting us, they are a source of inner freedom. Here is Pope Francis' explanation:

> They teach us how to avoid the slavery to which the many idols that we ourselves build reduce us.... They teach us to open ourselves to a wider dimension than the material one; to live with respect for others; overcoming the greed of power, possessions, and money; to be honest and sincere in our relationships; to protect all of creation and to nurture our planet with high, noble, and spiritual ideals. Following the Ten Commandments means being faithful to ourselves, to our most authentic nature, and walking towards the true freedom that Christ taught us in the Beatitudes.[4]

Richard T. De George, professor of Philosophy and Business Administration, endorses the commandments from a business ethics prospective:

> In a broad sense, ethics in business is simply the application of everyday moral or ethical norms in business. Perhaps the example from the Bible that comes to mind most readily is the Ten Commandments, a guide that is still used by many today. In particular, the injunctions to truthfulness and honesty or the prohibition against theft and envy are directly applicable.[5]

In addition to the Judeo-Christian religious traditions, other major religions and philosophies have 'moral road maps' – for example, the Five Pillars of Islam, the Eightfold Path and the Four Noble Truths of Buddhism, and its Ten Great Precepts, which prohibit lying and stealing and promote generosity and harmony.[6]

It is clear that the lessons and values inherent in the Ten Commandments are just as relevant today as they were in the time of Moses and the Israelite people.

These values are found at the heart of who we are as children of God, of the quest for human rights, the right to life and the sustainability of the planet.

King David learned the value of the Divine law. The following words are an excellent reminder of how much we need God's law for our well-being.

> The law of the Lord is perfect, refreshing the soul;
> The decree of the Lord is trustworthy, giving wisdom
>   to the simple;
> The precepts of the Lord are right, rejoicing the heart;
> The command of the Lord is clear, enlightening the eye ...
> The ordinances of the Lord are true, all of them just;
> They are more precious than gold, than a heap of purest gold;
> Sweeter also than syrup or honey from the comb.
> (Psalm 19:8-11)[7]

I

The First Commandment

I am the Lord your God;
you shall not have strange gods before me.
—*Exodus* 20:2-3

The recognition of one God distinguished the people of Israel from their pagan neighbours, who worshipped many deities. God's liberation of Israel from slavery in Egypt also made the people's relationship to God clear and meaningful. It was a call to love and honour the one true God above all else. The Hebrew Scriptures are replete with this theme.

The Lord in Zion is great, he is high above all the peoples ... (Psalm 99:2)

... the Lord is a great God, and a great king above all gods ... (Psalm 95:3)

Hear O Israel! The Lord is our God, the Lord alone! Therefore, you shall love the Lord, your God, with all your heart, and with all your soul, and with all your strength. (Deuteronomy 6:4-5)

The corollary to the first sentence of this commandment, then, is that we, God's creatures, are not to practise idolatry. Idols come in many forms. The most obvious are money, power, influence and materialism. We engage in idolatry when we give someone or something absolute value. This takes our primary focus off God and puts it on a creature.

Two practical examples of how this can occur have to do with religious life. One is from a friend of mine named Tom. After graduating from college, he told his parents that he was going to join the Society of Jesus (Jesuits). The effect of this news on his mother and father was interesting. His mother affirmed and encouraged him in his decision. However, his father became so enraged by the idea, he told Tom that if he went ahead with his plans, he would never speak to Tom again and would write him out of his will. This put Tom in a difficult position – should he follow the will of his earthly father or his heavenly Father?

Had Tom put 'absolute value' on his father and what his father wanted for him, he would have found another way of life. After praying more over his decision and seeking advice from a good friend, Tom decided to follow his heart and joined the Jesuits. For nine years, his father did not speak to him. Then, a year before his ordination, his father finally broke his silence and attended Tom's ordination.

The second story is my own. The realization of a vocation came to me out of the blue. I was 24 years old, had a full social life, was driving the car of my dreams (it was a silver blue Austin Healey convertible!) and had a very good job as a salesman for a food cannery. Plus, my father was waiting for me to get some experience in the food business (he was a successful food broker) and then go to work for him and eventually take over the family business. My idols were material things. Just thinking about the possibility of giving them up was a struggle. In fact, since the idea of being a Jesuit and a priest came so suddenly, when I decided to give it a try I asked my father if I could leave my car at his house. I asked him to keep it for six months and not sell it, in case the vocation didn't work out. If it didn't, I wanted the car back! That was over 50 years ago. As it turned out, God read my thoughts and gave me the grace to let go of everything in order to choose him instead.

In the early days of my Jesuit life, I read a poem by Francis Thompson, entitled "The Hound of Heaven," that clarified what had happened to me. The Hound is God; here is the excerpt that touched me:

> All which I took from thee I did but take,
> Not for thy harms,
> But just that thou might'st seek it in My arms.
> All which thy child's mistake
> Fancies as lost, I have stored for thee at home ...[1]

Have you found yourself, at times, putting 'absolute value' on something or someone other than God? It is very easy to do.

I think that one of the underlying causes of the Great Recession, which began in the United States in 2007, was the all-consuming desire on the part of some people to amass as much money as they could without regard for the adverse effect their actions would have on the lives of others. They lost their moral compass as they worshipped the almighty dollar, which is the opposite of living the first commandment.

A prayer exercise that many have found helpful in keeping the first commandment is called "Principle and Foundation." It comes from the Spiritual Exercises of St. Ignatius of Loyola, a retreat manual. At the beginning of this meditation, Ignatius proposes that the primary purpose of our life is to live in such a way in this life that we will live with God forever. However, he acknowledges that obstacles can derail our objective. These he calls "disordered attachments," which is another way of saying 'idols.' Here is a modern translation of Ignatius on this point:

> All the things in this world are gifts of God ... we appreciate and use these gifts insofar as they help us develop as loving persons. But if any of these gifts become the center of our lives, they displace God and so hinder our growth towards our goal.[2]

Ignatius then offers a prayer-remedy for dealing with these distractions.

In everyday life, then, we must hold ourselves in balance before all these created gifts insofar as we have a choice and are not bound by some obligation. We should not fix our desires on health or sickness, wealth or poverty, success or failure, a long life or a short one. For everything has the potential of calling forth in us a deeper response to our life in God.[3]

Someone who exemplifies this understanding of the first commandment is Tom Miller. Tom and his wife, Carmen, moved from San Francisco to Las Vegas after each earned their college degree. Tom studied psychology; Carmen, economics. Earlier, when Tom was in the US Air Force, he served as the chaplain's assistant. In Las Vegas, God took this young man of 27 and guided him away from a job in one of the hotel-casinos to what is known as Catholic Charities, an organization dedicated to providing basic services to those most in need in the community. Tom began as a volunteer, then became a paid staff member, and eventually was appointed executive director, a post he held for 23 years. "I felt led by the Holy Spirit from the Air Force on," he told me.

I asked Tom about raising a family in Las Vegas – he and Carmen have three sons and a daughter – where temptations to sex, gambling and greed are more obvious than in most cities. He said that he and Carmen were well aware of the moral challenges for their children, and so as parents they strongly emphasized solid Christian values. Their efforts paid off.

Three of their children were valedictorians at the local Catholic high school; another was senior class president. "Each has done well in their profession," Tom said, "and each still practises their faith. We have been blessed." Tom and Carmen use their gifts in service of God and of the community. Their ongoing focus on the divine in their personal and professional lives is an inspiration to all who know them.

The first commandment embraces three values: faith, trust and commitment.

Faith

This is faith in "a power greater than ourselves," as Alcoholics Anonymous states its in the Twelve Steps – faith in a God of unconditional love who cares for us and for our spiritual welfare. Our responsibility is to nourish and protect this faith and to treat anything that is opposed to it as rubbish.

Trust

Trust goes to the core of this commandment. It involves a kind of abandonment to the love of God. Charles de Foucauld, a spiritual writer and priest of the Sahara Desert, expressed this sentiment well in this prayer:

> Father, I abandon myself into your hands:
> do with me what you will.
> Whatever you may do I thank you:
> I am ready for all, I accept all.
>
> Let only your will be done in me,
> and in all your creatures.
> I wish no more than this, O Lord.
>
> Into your hands I commend my soul:
> I offer it you
> with all the love of my heart,
> for I love you, Lord,
> and so need to give myself,
> to surrender myself into your hands,
> without reserve,
> and with boundless confidence,
> for you are my Father.[4]

This was a man steeped in the theology of the first commandment. His words are both inspiring and challenging.

When I think of trust in my own life, I recall the times God has asked me to move from a place I dearly loved to one I had never lived in before or even thought of living in. After 15 years in the

San Francisco-Berkeley Bay Area, where Jesuits were plentiful and thus community life was full, I moved to San Diego, to a parish in the inner city and a small Jesuit community. The reason I felt inclined to move to the south was so that I could easily travel back and forth across the border to Tijuana, Mexico. I had lived in this border city for a summer and had fallen in love with the people. I wanted to minister to them as much as I could. However, this move meant leaving the many people I had come to love in the Bay Area.

I came to the inner freedom to make the move the day I meditated on the story of the rich young man in the Gospel of Matthew (19:16-21). The young man in the story, who had been keeping the commandments to the best of his ability, asked Jesus what he needed to do to grow deeper in his faith. Jesus responded: "If you seek perfection, go, sell your possessions, and give to the poor. You will then have treasure in heaven." I asked myself, "What do I *have* and what do I need to let go of in order to move?" The answer was the beauty of the Bay area, the many Jesuit friends I had there, and the many sisters and lay people I had come to know; none of these were easy to let go of. Had my ultimate focus been on the place and people of northern California instead of on God and what he wanted, I would not have been able to move. This decision to move also involved answering a second question: "What do I have to *give* to the poor (of Tijuana)?" The answer was simple: "my time and my love." I did move and stayed in San Diego for 16 years, 14 of which involved ministering in a small parish in an economically poor section of Tijuana. I was profoundly blessed by the many wonderful people I met in what is known as Colonia Esperanza – "district of hope."

My next experience of abandoning myself to God's wishes involved a severe climate change – from one of the best year-round climates in the world, San Diego, to Cluny, Alberta, Canada, and its very cold winters. Cluny is in the middle of the prairies and is located an hour and a half east of Calgary. This move also meant going from ministering among Mexican people to a new culture for me: First Nations people. Moving from San Diego to the Reserve took more courage than the one from the Bay Area to San Diego, because for the first time in my life I was to live alone and for an extended time. Frankly, I had a fear of living alone.[5]

I remained on the Siksika Reserve for almost two years. Because living on the prairies was an isolating experience for me, my prayer for the first couple of months can be summed up in one word: "Help!" Southern Alberta continued to be my home for seven more years, in Calgary.

Complete trust in God was what I needed for these two moves, plus a boost of grace to my generosity and courage.

Have you had a similar experience of radical change in your life?

Perhaps it was in the form of a change of location or job. Whatever the adjustment, you might find the following prayer-reflection by Thomas Flowers helpful, as I have. It is called "I Say Yes to God," and is an ideal prayer for the first commandment.

First you said,
Let's sail into uncharted waters
Without so much as a compass
And I hesitatingly said,
Well, as long as you're there.

Then you said,
Lose the life preserver
And cut the anchor,
And I said
If you say so.
Then you said,
Abandon the ship
For the lifeboat
And forget the oars.
And I said,
All right.

Then, just this morning, you said,
Let go of the rudder,
Sit easy and smile,
And don't worry about knowing
Where we're going, because I do.
And I said,
Yes.[6]

Commitment

The first commandment – "I am the Lord your God … You shall not have other gods beside me" (Exodus 20) – invites us to an examination of consciousness. Who or what is the primary focus of my life? M. Basilea Schlink offers us a helpful outline for this reflective exercise. It is called "A Look into Your Heart."

What could your idol be?
Anything that you value more than God –
even though it may be good in itself –
for this takes His place in your life.
Anything that you prefer to God,
whom you are called to love above all else.

Your work, your career –
No time for God.

Your reputation, your status –
No honor for God.

Your family, wife, husband or child –
God does not have first place in your life.

Your house, your home –
Instead of treasure in heaven.

Your vacations, your travels –
Instead of time spent with God.

Your health, your appearance.
Every earthly thing that devalues for you
the divine gifts received through fellowship
with God.

Everything that is more important to you
than the Lord.[7]

We nurture commitment in three ways: through prayer, discipline and acts of integrity.

Prayer keeps us growing in relationship/friendship with the Lord. Prayer also expands our capacity for hope. According to the *Catechism of the Catholic Church*, "the first commandment summons us to believe in God, to hope in God, and to love God above all else" (CCC no. 2134). We also need to pray to discern idols when they appear.

Discipline is needed in order to say "No" to temptations to put absolute value on a created thing, especially when the person or object is very appealing. Discipline involves self-knowledge, both about our inner strengths and about the kind of morally unhealthy desires we can have in the abuse of power, prestige, status, sexuality or success.

Acts of integrity consist of doing the right thing for the right reasons, even at personal cost. This virtue is the opposite of what might be called 'moral laziness.'

The first commandment requires a commitment to integrity so we can keep our focus on God and on the values of the gospel in a consistent way. Integrity and moral courage go hand in hand.

The first commandment is the foundation for the other nine.

2

The Second Commandment

You shall not take the name of the Lord your God in vain.
—*Exodus* 20:7

As noted in the Introduction, Fr. Ian Knox, in his book *Theology for Teachers*, suggests that we look at the commandments not only in their negative form, but also in their positive form.[1] The positive form of the first commandment would be "Recognize, accept and worship only the One, True God." The second commandment in its positive form would be "Respect and reverence God" – which includes God's name.

It is important to spend some time considering the word "name." The noted scripture scholar John L. McKenzie reminds us that it is commonly accepted that a person's name is considered to be more than an artificial tag that distinguishes one individual from another.[2] A name has a mysterious identity with its bearer; it can even be considered a substitute for the person, as acting or receiving in his or her place. A name is thought to tell us something of the kind of person he or she is. I found this to be especially true among First Nations people in southern Alberta, where for many their last name is directly connected to their birth, clan or personality.

While I lived among the Blackfoot people, I was given a spiritual name: "Eagle Head." When I asked the late Greg Running

Rabbit, who conferred the name upon me, why he had chosen it, he responded that the eagle is the creature closest to the Creator, as it flies higher than any other bird. In my role as parish administrator, he continued, I was seen by the parish as representing God to the people.

To show disrespect or to insult another's name is seen as insulting the person. The second commandment is an admonition against doing just that in relation to God. How important is God's name? Psalm 8 proclaims:

> O Lord, our God, how glorious is your name over all the earth!
> You have exalted your majesty above the heavens. (8:1)

God confides his name to those who believe in him; this conferring implies intimacy and trust. For this reason it should not be abused.[3] Respect for God's name is an expression of the respect we owe to the mystery that is the essence of God.

In addition, God calls each of us by name, which makes each person's name sacred. Consider the following passage from the prophet Isaiah:

> But now, thus says the Lord, who created you, O Jacob and formed you, O Israel [in *praying* the Bible, substitute your name for "Jacob" and "Israel"]:
> Fear not for I have redeemed you;
> I have called you by name: you are mine. (43:1)

The divine name, McKenzie explains, has all the significance and power of the human name raised to a fitting degree.[4]

There are many descriptions of God – creator, sustainer, liberator, healer, provider and law-giver, to name only a few. It is helpful to reflect on our own image of God.[5] On retreats, I often ask the participants three questions:

- What was your image of God when you were a child?
- Has your image of God changed over the years?
- Do any passages from the Bible speak to you in a special way of the personal love of God?

To the first question, I add these questions:

- Can you recall any particular attributes or characteristics of God that you learned when you were a child?
- How was your family influential in shaping your image of God?
- Were there any special religious symbols in your home that were meaningful to you?

To the second question, I add these:

- What are the characteristics of God that are especially meaningful to you now?
- If your image of God has changed over the years, what do you attribute this to? For example, a person, an event, a grace, an insight?

This is an important exercise, because the answers say a lot about how you view yourself and others, as well as how you relate to God.

In my early life, I experienced God mainly as a law-giver – and a strict one, at that. The Second Vatican Council (1962–1965) and its teachings on a God of love and mercy helped change my perception of God to one of unconditional love. This realization affected me both emotionally and spiritually. Emotionally, my self-esteem underwent a radical transformation, from low to an inner acceptance and peace. Spiritually, I gained a different perspective on loving my neighbour as I love myself. Eventually, this translated into my interest in morality and ethical behaviour in the business world, which is another way of promoting the Name of God. Morality begins with God loving us and our accepting this love. Living it out is in the realm of ethics. The fact that I come from a family of business people and was in business before I joined the Jesuits also helped me choose this focus.

Protecting One's Name

Christians believe that human beings are made in the image and likeness of God; that explains why the dignity of the human person is one of the main pillars of Christian moral theology. Combine this truth with God calling each of us by name (Isaiah 43:1) and we have an imperative to protect our name. This has become especially evident in recent years, with the danger of identity theft. But our name and thus our self can be harmed in other ways, as well. Here are some.

In the course of my work in ethics, I met a very interesting man by the name of Hank Shea a few years ago. Hank is a former Assistant US attorney who prosecuted hundreds of white-collar offenders – including bankers, lawyers, business owners and executives – from companies large and small.[6] Based on his experience, he identified 10 of the most important lessons to be learned from the misconduct and wrongdoing of others. I will be quoting Hank a number of times in this book, but for the topic at hand, here is Lesson No. 9 (the lessons begin at No. 10 and go to No. 1):

Never knowingly sign a false document.

No matter what type of document is at issue – expense account, stock option, tax return – it is almost always a crime and it is always wrong to intentionally sign an official document that is untrue or inaccurate. Your word and your signature are your bond; consequently, you should never put them at risk by stretching the truth or endorsing something that you know is not right. Your signature is also permanent: It often outlives your memory, and may even outlive you. Therefore, always sign your name with care.[7]

You can also 'prostitute' your name by *perjury*. If you find yourself in a courtroom in the United States and are sworn in, you pledge to "tell the truth, the whole truth, and nothing but the truth, so help me God." In other countries, you must swear an oath or make an affirmation that you will be truthful. The second commandment forbids false oaths, because taking an oath or swearing is to take God as witness to what you are affirming. According to the *Catechism of the Catholic Church*, to invoke the divine truthfulness as pledge of one's own truthfulness engages the Lord's name. We have a duty towards God to avoid false oaths, because a false oath calls on God to be witness to a lie. A person is guilty of *perjury* when he or she makes a promise under oath with no intention of keeping it, or when after promising on oath he or she does not keep the promise. This kind of pledging is contrary to the holiness of the divine name (CCC nos. 2150, 2151, 2152, 2154). An oath, according to the second commandment, can call on the divine name only as a witness, unless in truth and in justice.

It may happen that an illegitimate authority demands an oath from you; obviously, you do not have to comply. In fact, you must refuse to do so. Jesus has something to say about such a situation:

> They will seize and persecute you, they will hand you over to the synagogues and to prisons and they will have you led before kings and governors because of my name. It will lead to your giving testimony. Remember, you are not to prepare your defense beforehand, for I myself shall give you a wisdom in speaking that all your adversaries will be powerless to resist or refute.... You will be hated by all because of my name, but not a hair on your head will be destroyed. By your perseverance you secure your lives. (Luke 21:12-19)

The second commandment forbids the abuse of the name of Jesus, the Father, and the Blessed Mother, as well as all the saints (CCC no. 2146).

Our Baptismal Name

What's in a name? Recall that in ancient Hebrew culture, the name was the person. To show respect to the name of a person was to show respect to the person.

We baptize in the *name* of the Father, and of the Son, and of the Holy Spirit. My baptismal name is George Joseph Oliva III. And that is who I am. However, shortly after I was born, the doctor had my fingernails taped and I was, so they say, "chunky." This led one of my uncles, who came to the hospital to see me with my father, to remark that I looked like Max Baer, who was then heavyweight boxing champion of the world. I was nicknamed "Max" and was never called anything else. "Max" is also who I am.

Patrick Twohy, in his insightful book *Finding a Way Home: Indian and Catholic Spiritual Paths of the Plateau Tribes*, writes that when we make the Sign of the Cross, we are calling God "the Holy Mystery, the One at the Center, and the Origin of all things."[8] About the Father, he writes:

> We call the Life within all things, the Energy moving from within, and the Breath of all that is born and lives; about the Son: It is He who gives us all things good, lasting, beautiful, His Bread is Life for us; and about the Holy Spirit: We call the Spirit the Presence, the One coming towards us in Love and Forgiveness.[9]

In expressing gratitude to God for his many blessings, the Prophet Isaiah proclaims:

> Give thanks to the Lord, acclaim his name;
> among the nations make known his deeds,
> proclaim how exalted is his name. (12:3-4)

The name of God is a source of protection for the believer, giving us freedom from fear and giving us the courage we need to do what God asks of us (Isaiah 12:2).

Christians say the name of God so often, it becomes second nature. The *Catechism of the Catholic Church* shows how:

> The Christian begins his [her] day, his [her] prayers, and his [her] activities with the Sign of the Cross: 'In the name of the Father and of the Son and of the Holy Spirit. Amen.' The baptized person dedicates the day to the glory of God and calls on the Savior's grace which lets him/her act in the Spirit as a child of the Father. The sign of the cross strengthens us in temptations and difficulties. (CCC no. 2157)

Hallowing God's Name

In the book of Sirach (Ecclesiasticus), the author extols Israel's great ancestors. All were glorious in their time, he writes, and adds, "Their bodies are peacefully laid away, but their name lives on and on" (44:14). I found a modern translation of this thought in the Entrance Antiphon of the Mass for January 2, 2013: "Let the peoples recount the wisdom of the Saints and let the Church proclaim their praise. Their names live on and on."[10] Let's remove the capital "s" from "saints" and think about those people we know or have known whose lives are so extraordinary that it is clear their name will live on long after they have died. And let's open our eyes to see the saints among us, who inspire us by who they are and what they do for the betterment of others. We might say, in the words of the Lord's Prayer, that they 'hallow' (honour) God's name in a special way. I have in mind two people in particular – Marlene Richter and Tracy Tomiak.

I first met Marlene at St. Christopher's Church, in North Las Vegas, Nevada, where she is a lector at one of the Sunday Masses. I was immediately impressed by her kindness to me and to others. I was new to the parish and she went out of her way to make sure I felt welcome. I was to discover that she is the Executive Director of a local organization – Shade Tree, which is a shelter for homeless and abused women and children in crisis. The vision of Shade Tree is self-reliance for every woman and child. As I have come to know Marlene, I have learned some of what motivated her to pursue a vocation in social work. Like many of us, she learned compassion as a child from her own experience of being mistreated. At the age of nineteen, the Lord found her, and she has been doing her best to follow in his footsteps ever since.

"Every once in a while," she said, "I ask God, 'what do you want me to do?'" The overall answer to this question has been to work with people who do not have a voice in society. Her goal is to create a culture of compassion, a vision, it seems to me, that has its source in her experience of being loved by God unconditionally. This vision is expressed well in Shade Tree's "statements of belief":

- That no one should ever have to endure a state of home-lessness, existing in fear for personal safety and without the means to meet even the most basic of human needs – food and shelter.
- That every human being, regardless of social status, has the right to be treated with dignity and respect.
- That all homeless children are victims because they lack choice and mobility.
- That homelessness is a community problem that impacts everyone.
- That everyone can be a part of the solution.[11]

By continually seeking what God wishes of her, and by follow-ing the Lord's lead by reaching out to those in society who are most in need of love and assistance, Marlene truly hallows God's name.

Tracy Tomiak lives in Calgary, Alberta, Canada. She is mar-ried and is the mother of five children. As a result of a terrible auto accident, she has suffered chronic pain for over 10 years. At the beginning of her ordeal, the Lord spoke to her and gave her the strength and the wisdom to move forward day by day. He told her that his love is greater than human weakness and limitation and that he would work wonders through her despite her infirmity. One very effective way he has done this is through a book Tracy wrote on her experience: *Thriving, Not Just Surviving: Living Abundantly with Pain*. In the Introduction to the book, she writes: "By asking for Christ's strength each moment, I discovered that I could be who He was calling me to be, despite my limitations. I stopped yearn-ing to return to my old self, and began to love the person Christ was transforming."[12]

A proficient multi-tasker before the accident, she learned how to put aside her pride and ask for help. Faced with her unsought and unexpected circumstances, Tracy writes:

Somewhere along my journey with chronic pain, I realized that I was not going to get back the time I was spending in pain. This is reality and it is my life. I had two choices: adapt to what Christ was allowing in my life, experiencing it as a journey with many lessons for me and those around me; or be bitter, angry and unforgiving.[13]

By choosing the former, Tracy hallows Christ's Name in a very special way: the same Christ who gave his life that we might have the inner strength we need to carry whatever cross comes our way; the same Christ who gave his life that we might know how to live.

The Power of Christ's Name

In his book *Jesus of Nazareth: The Infancy Narratives*, Pope Benedict XVI considers the following passage from John's Gospel (The Prologue) to make a profound point about the power of Christ's name: "For to all who received him, who believed in his name, he gave power to become children of God; who were born not of blood nor of the will of the flesh nor of the will of man, but of God" (1:12f; RSV).

The Pope explains that those who believe in Christ's name receive a new origin through that name. He writes:

> those who believe in Jesus enter through faith into Jesus' unique new origin, and they receive this origin as their own. In and of themselves, all these believers are initially 'born of blood and of the will of man.' But their faith gives them a new birth: they enter into the origin of Jesus Christ, which now becomes their own origin. From Christ, through faith in him, they are now born of God.[14]

This is a short summary of our spiritual genealogy: faith in Jesus and in his name. He gives us a new origin, an origin that comes from God.

3

The Third Commandment

Remember to keep holy the Lord's Day.
—*Exodus* 20:8-9

I grew up in a traditional Catholic family. Sunday Mass was a given in our home, and central to our faith. Church was not only a place of prayer for us, but also a source of community. Many of my lifelong friends belonged to the same parish as I did. My mother was a member of the St. Vincent de Paul Society at the parish; she was an inspiration to me of how to put one's faith into action for those in need. Admittedly, in high school I easily became distracted during Mass, but it never occurred to me not to attend. Mass was in Latin when I was a youth, the priest faced away from the people, there was no sharing of peace, and we knelt at the communion rail to receive the Eucharist.

I joined the Jesuits in 1962, at the age of 24. I had no idea at the time that the Second Vatican Council had begun the same year. At the end of our two-year Novitiate, many liturgical changes took place in the Church: Mass was in the vernacular, the priest faced the people, the people offered one another a sign of peace, and the communion rails disappeared.

The primary emphasis seemed to shift from mystery (fostered by the Latin language) to having a personal relationship with God.

This change suited me just fine, because I had come to realize the personal and unconditional love of God while I was in the Novitiate.

Sabbath and the Lord's Day

To fully understand and appreciate the third commandment, we need to look at its origin. The theological basis of taking a day of rest (SBT, or *Sabbat*, in Hebrew) is that this is what God did after he fashioned creation. In the Bible, we read, "Since on the seventh day God was finished with the work he had been doing, he rested on the seventh day from all the work he had undertaken" (Genesis 2:3). John McKenzie writes that from early Israelite times, the Sabbath was a holy day marked by religious and probably some kind of cultic observance.[1] Scripture scholar E.P. Sanders points out that Jewish self-understanding focused first and foremost on their gracious election by God as God's covenant people; this was how Jewish people entered into their special relationship with God. The Law was understood as the God-given means by which the people maintained or stayed in their covenant relationship with God.[2]

The fullest form of the third commandment is found in the Book of Deuteronomy:

> Take care to keep holy the Sabbath day as the Lord your God commanded you. Six days you may labour and do all your work; but the seventh day is the Sabbath of the Lord, your God. No work may be done then, whether by you, or your son or daughter, or your male or female slave, or your ox or ass or any of your beasts, or the alien who lives with you. (5:12-14a)

The Sabbath reveals a memorial of Israel's liberation from slavery in Egypt. Therefore, it is a sacred day, a sign of the covenant. Its meaning is captured well in these words: "The Sabbath is for the Lord, holy and set apart for the praise of God, his work of creation, and his saving actions on behalf of Israel" (CCC no. 2171).

Whereas the Jewish Sabbath is observed on Saturday, the Christian honouring of the third commandment is on Sunday. This change goes back to the earliest days of Christianity and has its theological basis in the resurrection, which occurred on the first day of the week – Sunday.

"After the Sabbath, as the first day of the week was dawning, Mary Magdalene came with the other Mary to inspect the tomb" (Matthew 28:1). An angel appears and tells them that Jesus has risen from the dead. The angel says, "Do not be frightened … Jesus has been raised from the dead and now goes ahead of you to Galilee, where you will see him" (28:5-7a).

Sunday is called "The Lord's Day"; it symbolizes the new creation brought about by Christ's rising from the dead. German theologian Jürgen Moltmann shows the connection between the Old Testament and the New by pointing out that whereas the Sabbath allows us to look back thankfully at the work of creation, the Christian celebration of the resurrection opens the outlook into the future of the new creation.[3]

Sunday liturgy is at the heart of the life of the Church and of her believers. The *Catechism of the Catholic Church* explains: "The celebration of Sunday observes the moral commandment inscribed by nature in the human heart to render to God an outward, visible, public, and regular worship 'as a sign of God's universal beneficence to all'" (CCC no. 2176). Believers gather together in faith and charity, witnesses to one another of their commitment to the values of the gospel. We need encouragement to live those values during the next week at school, work, play or any social situation in which we find ourselves. Our Anglican brothers and sisters write of the Christian life as an adventure, a voyage of discovery, a journey sustained by faith and hope.

> To be a Christian means that, whatever one's state, the journey goes on. It is staking everything on the belief that this way of using our one and only life will in the end be validated not only as the best for our human condition but as most truly in accord with ultimate reality.[4]

To be sure, our personal prayers away from church are extremely important and effective. However, there is an added grace given to us when we gather with others to acknowledge our common humanity, listen to God's word, receive the Eucharist, and experience a sending forth to make the world a better place by our faith-filled presence. Frank Halfmoon of the Cayuse Nez Percé Nation sums up this idea well: "Praying by ourselves is necessary, but when many pray together, the voice is strong."[5]

Some Personal Reflections

I was ordained to the priesthood over 40 years ago. Since that time, I have had the privilege of presiding at the Sunday liturgy in a variety of parishes, mainly in the United States, Mexico and Canada. I have also been graced by a number of different cultures. In addition to my own, I have celebrated Mass in African American, Filipino, First Nations and Hispanic (in Spanish) parishes. I have felt emotionally and spiritually enriched by each culture. Currently, I celebrate Sunday liturgies in two parishes. At St. Christopher, where I live, the composition of the parish is mostly Hispanic, but there are also Caucasian, African American and Asian parishioners. At the other parish, Christ the King, God graces me with a youth Mass and a Mass in Spanish.

There are two graces in particular related to the Eucharist that have had a significant impact on my priesthood. The first occurred about five years after I was ordained. I was making my annual retreat. I decided to ask God for a deeper feeling for the Eucharist. After all, I had been presiding at Mass for five years and I didn't want it to become routine. After asking for the grace, I dropped into a spiritual darkness that lasted a couple of days.

The priest I was seeing each day of the retreat asked me how things were going. I told him, "Terrible. I am in some kind of deep darkness."

He asked, "What did you pray for?"

I told him. He said, "Well, you got it, but you got the passion part of the Eucharist."

I exclaimed, "But I was looking for the resurrection part!"

To which he sagely responded, "Watch out what you pray for!"

The Eucharist is indeed an experience of both the passion and the resurrection of Jesus; both sacrifice and new life. Pope John Paul II explained this truth in his encyclical letter *Ecclesia de Eucharistia*:

> By virtue of its close relationship to the sacrifice of Golgotha, the Eucharist is *a sacrifice in the strict sense* ... The gift of [Christ's] love and obedience to the point of giving his life is in the first place a gift to his Father. Certainly it is a gift given for our sake, and indeed that of all humanity, yet it is *first and foremost a gift to the Father:* "a sacrifice that the Father accepted, giving, in return for this total self-giving by his Son, who 'became obedient unto death,' his own paternal gift, that is to say the grant of new immortal life in the resurrection".[6]

The second grace happened during one Sunday Mass while I was giving out holy communion. Priests, deacons and ministers of communion can get into a rhythm as they say to each person, "The Body of Christ." As I said this to one of the persons in line, the insight that everyone coming to communion and everyone in the Church *is* the Body of Christ became clearer to me than ever before. The realization came in a flash, but it has stayed with me ever since.

The spiritual significance of the Mass cannot be overstated. Christians believe that Christ is present in many places, but above all in the living sacrament of his body and blood. Rev. Lawrence Mick points out that there are four modes of Christ's presence in the Mass: in the assembly, in the presider, in the word and in the meal.[7]

In the Assembly – "Where two or three are gathered in my Name, there I am in their midst" (Matthew 18:20). We are enriched by the faith and commitment of those present.

In the Presider – The true leader of our worship is, of course, Jesus; he invites us to share in the Eucharist through his human representative. Fortunately, this person does not have to be perfect. According to St. Paul, it is in the weakness of being human that the efficacy of Christ's priesthood lies (Hebrews 5:1-3).

In the Word – When the word of God is proclaimed at Mass, Christ is truly speaking to us in and through the gospel. The Spirit also speaks to us in the other readings. As a homilist, it is especially meaningful to me to connect one or more of the other readings and even the psalm to the gospel. I enjoy preaching very much and will forever be grateful to Fr. Frank Fawcett of the San Diego Diocese, who encouraged me to bring appropriate accounts of my own faith story into my homilies.

Over the years, countless men, women and even teenagers have commented positively on this practice. I remember one man at a parish where I was giving a mission; he made an appointment to see me privately. He wanted to share a significant part of his life story with me, something that he had not shared with anyone else, including his family. When I asked him why he decided to do this during the mission, he said, "After hearing you share some of your story, I felt I could trust you with mine."

In the Meal – In *Ecclesia de Eucharistia*, Pope John Paul II wrote:

> The Eucharist is indelibly marked by the event of the Lord's passion and death ... The sacramental re-presentation of Christ's sacrifice, crowned by the resurrection, in the Mass involves a most special presence which is called 'real' ... it is a presence in the fullest sense: a substantial presence whereby Christ is wholly and entirely present.[8]

This "substantial presence" is what gives the receiver the kind of spiritual nourishment he or she needs for closer union with God and the grace to go forth from the Mass to live the gospel the rest of the week. According to St. Paul, holiness is being more and more conformed into the likeness of Jesus – putting on his mind and heart: "love, joy, peace, patient endurance, kindness, generosity, faith, mildness and chastity" (Galatians 5:22-23). This is what it is to live by the Spirit. This is what it is to love one's neighbour as oneself.

"Go Forth and Spread the Good News":
The Vertical and the Horizontal Dimensions of Faith

"Keeping holy the Sabbath day" has moral implications for how we live out our faith the other six days of the week. The vertical dimension of our spirituality, which is prayer and the sacraments, must find expression in the horizontal dimension, which includes good works and ethical conduct in our daily life. As Alice Walker, author of *The Color Purple*, puts it so well, "Anybody can observe the Sabbath, but making it holy surely takes the rest of the week."[9] And the late businessman Oskar Ernst Bernhardt (1875–1941), who was also an essayist and reflective thinker, had this to say on the third commandment:

> No one keeps an hour of rest holy by going to church, unless at the same time during the time of rest he or she is prepared to reflect on what they have heard there, in order to absorb it rightly deep within and live accordingly. The priest cannot make your day holy for you if you do not do so of yourself. Consider carefully ever again whether the real sense of the Word of God is completely in accord with your activity.[10]

A significant part of my ministry since 2002 has been with men and women in the corporate community, first in Calgary, Alberta, and now in Las Vegas. The focus of this ministry is the intimate connection between spirituality and ethics.[11] One of the resources I use comes from the CFA Institute (Chartered Financial Analyst) and its "Integrity List." Here are 11 of the 50 recommendations from the list: suggestions on how to live our faith at work in practical and meaningful ways.

- Commit to a gold standard code of ethics and professional conduct.
- Act with integrity 24/7 – not just at the office.
- Lead by example with your firm and colleagues.
- Advocate for stronger regulations that protect investors.
- Write articles and speak publicly about ethics.

- Act with fairness and prudence with every decision.
- Always be honest with clients.
- Vocally demand that your firm does what is right for clients.
- Promote the concept of earning money rather than making money.
- Bring an ethical dimension to discussions of business strategy.
- Remind junior associates that reputations are hard earned and easily lost.[12]

An image that speaks clearly of the integration of the vertical and the horizontal dimensions of our faith comes from a statue of Jesus that I saw in front of a church. Vandals had broken the hands of Jesus. I was told that the pastor deliberated on whether to have the statue repaired. In the end, he decided not to. Instead, he placed a plaque at the base of the statue that reads "I have no hands but yours."

These words echo a prayer of St. Teresa of Avila (1515–1582):

Christ has no body now, but yours.
No hands, no feet on earth, but yours.
Yours are the eyes through which he looks
With compassion on this world.

Let nothing disturb you.
Let nothing frighten you.
All things pass away: God never changes.
Patience obtains all things.
Those who have God
Find they lack nothing;
God alone suffices.[13]

We are the hands and heart of the Lord at work, at school, at play, everywhere. We honour God by keeping the Sabbath holy and living it in our daily lives.

4

The Fourth Commandment

Honour your father and mother.
—*Exodus* 20:12

The first three commandments point us in the direction of our creaturehood, in light of the Creator's personal love for us. The other seven point to Jesus' words to his disciples: "Love one another even as I have loved you" (John 13:34). These commandments refer to our interpersonal relationships.

The fourth commandment is primarily addressed to children (of all ages) in their relationship to their parents, because this is the most fundamental and universal unit. As it says in the *Catechism of the Catholic Church*, "God has willed that, after him, we should honor our parents to whom we owe life and who have handed on to us the knowledge of God" (CCC no. 2197). Ideally, the primary virtues for this relationship are mutual respect, affection and gratitude. But what if one or even both parents are psychologically incapable of fulfilling their parental roles?

To bring this possibility of a dysfunctional relationship with one or more parents into the practical arena, here is my experience. My mother and I had a close friendship as I was growing up, especially when I was in high school. She was my best friend. My father and I were on pretty good terms until I began my teenage years. Then he seemed to have two personalities, one friendly and humorous, the other sarcastic and demeaning. The most emotionally damaging of this 'split' was when he would put me down in front of my friends. 'Honouring' him was the last thing on my mind.

It took me a long time – into my late 20s – before I was able to live this commandment in relation to him. It was at that time that I confronted him about his unhealthy behaviour towards me. This became the turning point in our ability to mutually respect one another and to actually become friends.

There were three aids that led me to this event. First, with the support of a good counsellor, I was able to get in touch with how I had been damaged by my father and to grow beyond it. Second, a movie called *David and Lisa* helped me. The film is about two troubled teenagers who come from unhealthy home environments. In a conference with their counsellor, he tells them, "Parents have a right to be fallible." I remember the shock I felt when the truth of this statement hit me. It gave me a greater tolerance for human weakness and a desire to know why my father was the way he was. A third form of help came from an insight I read in a book about male psychology; the author made the point that there can be tension in a family between the eldest son (which I am) and the father because they are both in love with the same woman: the mother. The tension is especially acute if the father is insecure. Curiously, my father was very successful in business but often insecure at home.

Lest we 'moderns' think we are the only people who must deal with dysfunction in family life, consider the following analysis of some of the Bible's broken families:

> The personal and community stories of God's people depict virtually every form of human mistake and malfeasance against family members: rape, incest, lying, stealing, murder, betrayal, and solicitation for prostitution. The book of Genesis describes one deeply disturbed family after another. Adam and Eve have one son who has killed their other son. Attracted to Jacob, Leah sleeps with him on his wedding night and thus invalidates his

seven years of waiting to marry her sister Rachel. Abraham lies and risks prostituting his wife to save himself. Sarah gives her servant Hagar to Abraham and then abuses the servant for doing exactly what Sarah has asked Hagar to do – give Abraham a son.[1]

How to cope? How to move from disrespect to respect, from hurt to healing? Christine A. Adams offers a five-step process in her fine article, "Forgiving Your Parents for Not Being Perfect."

1. *Make a list of your hurts.* Get your hidden resentments out in the open and examine them, all the things you have resented about your parents. Your list should be specific. Not "I hate my father (or mother)," but "I resent that you never hugged me" or "that you never told me that you loved me." Strong feelings of anger, loss, hurt, may come up. Let them. (I bring what comes up to God for healing.)

2. *Use creative visualization to heal your hurts.* Once you have made a list of the hurtful incidents, visualize your parent hearing you state these resentments, acknowledging your pain, and accepting your feelings. The objective here is not to confront your parent but to clear the emotions out of your present life. Forgiveness does not need to happen in the actual presence of your parents, but it does need to happen within you.

3. *Write a letter and share it with a supportive person.* Address the letter to the parent who has hurt you. In this letter, that you will never deliver, you can get at the reality of your feelings. You can say things that you never would say in person. Simply start at the beginning and write. Then share your letter with a supportive person whom you trust implicitly – one who will not make comments or judgments, or try to fix everything for you. This step is essential to giving credibility to the problem and to furthering the process of healing.

4. *Give yourself the gift of forgiveness.* Our parents did the best they could with the knowledge, capabilities, and resources they

had. As God forgives us, God also forgives them. Whenever we hold back forgiveness, we show a need to hold on to our hidden resentments. Perhaps this allows us to live in the past and avoid the present. Our bitterness is like a cancer that grows from the inside out. By forgiving, we choose freedom and peace instead. Forgiveness is a gift to ourselves!

5. *Believe that you are first and foremost a child of God.* When we forgive our parents for not being perfect, we begin to recognize our own lovableness as children of God. No matter what our parents were like, we are not our parents. Even if we look like our parents, walk like them, and do some of the awful things they did, we have a separate spiritual self. We are of God. We are children of God first.[2]

Let us return to my family and our history. My father had good qualities, too. He taught me to be responsible by his example of working hard and supporting our family. Honesty was a key virtue that he and my mother instilled in us children. My father was a natural-born salesman; he passed this personality trait on to me. He and my mother were faithful Catholics and made sure my siblings and I got a proper Catholic education. I went to a Jesuit high school and a Jesuit university. I am grateful for these gifts and honour both of my parents with my prayers; both are deceased.

A year after my father died (one month shy of his 80th birthday), I saw a video interview by Bill Moyers with Robert Bly, author of *Iron John*, a book about the male psyche.[3] The interview affected me deeply, as I realized that although I had dealt with a lot of my father issues when I was in my late 20s (as described above), there were still some issues I had not yet dealt with. There were some hurts buried deep in my subconscious that had not yet been healed.

Bly maintains that an important door to male feeling is grief. Expressing grief for some men is difficult, because most of us were taught as children that it is not 'manly' to cry.

That was certainly true in my case. Dr. Alan Wolfelt, a respected grief counsellor and author, states it well:

As the boy moves toward becoming a man he is taught to behave in certain acceptable 'masculine' ways. Acknowledging feelings of loss in this context results in feelings of vulnerability and uncomfortableness.... The social conditioning process of glorified masculinity creates a major impediment to a male's expression of grief.[4]

As a result of the Bly interview, I came to the conclusion that if I was to fully honour my father according to the fourth commandment, I would have to find ways to grieve whatever unhealed hurts remained in my psyche. This I was able to do over a period of time. I wrote about this in my 1997 book *The Masculine Spirit: Resources for Reflective Living*, in Chapter 7, "Dealing with Father Wounds."[5] Many men over the years have told me how helpful that chapter has been for their emotional growth. I have been amazed by the number of women who have told me the same thing about their need to be healed of an emotional hurt administered by a man or, in some cases, by their mother or another female adult.

Part II: Civil Society

The fourth commandment also applies to civil society: those who exercise authority towards those they serve and those who are served toward authorities. Each is to honour and respect the other. Of course, this applies only to legitimate authority.

However, even in a situation where authority is legitimate, due to free and open elections and judicious appointments, honouring those in authority presents a challenge for some people. For example, in the 1960s, in the United States, it was common among college students to automatically question authority. There was even a bumper sticker that advocated this message. In addition, there are those who believe the government is too involved in people's lives and who rebel against what they perceive as intrusion. Then there are the various scandals – some in the marital arena – among some politicians, which leaves the populace skeptical and cynical about the political scene. Finally, there has been a non-compromising attitude in the US Congress on the part of both those on the far left and those on the far right of the political spectrum that leaves little room for mutual honour and respect.

The *Catechism of the Catholic Church* outlines the duties of both civil authorities and citizens:

Civil authorities

- respect the rights of each person regardless of race, nationality, creed, sexual orientation, and economic status
- honour a just hierarchy of values
- value the common good over personal interest
- facilitate the exercise of freedom and responsibility by all
- place a high value on service
- practice distributive justice
- live an ethical life both in one's personal life and in one's occupation.
  (CCC nos. 2234–2237)

Citizens

- respect legitimate leaders
- contribute to the good of society in a spirit of truth, justice, solidarity, and freedom
- love and serve one's country
- pay taxes
- exercise the right to vote
- defend one's country
- follow the right of conscience: obliged not to follow any directives of civil authorities that are contrary to the moral order, to the fundamental rights of persons, or to the teachings of the gospel.
  (CCC nos. 2238–2243)

Since immigration is a hot topic these days, it is worth mentioning that immigrants are obliged to respect with gratitude the material and spiritual heritage of the country that receives them, to obey its laws and to assist in carrying civic burdens (CCC no. 2241).

Part III: The World of Business

A third reality that this commandment refers to is the relationship of employers and employees. I am indebted to the input of two friends for this section – businessmen John Laub and Jim Lamb, both of Las Vegas – and two authors, John R. Boatright and J.-Robert Ouimet.

Boatright points out that every person in a business enterprise occupies a role. "A role is a structured set of relationships with accompanying rights and obligations ... In occupying a role, a person assumes certain rights that are not held by everyone as well as certain role-specific obligations."[6] Thus, the obligations of the board of directors are different from those of a manager, who has different responsibilities from those he or she manages, and so on.

Considering roles in a general way, employers need to respect their employees, and vice versa. Employers must not treat their employees as merely a means to an end or as ciphers, but as valued men and women in a common enterprise, the company. They must give good ethical example. If the company is in financial trouble, honesty about the situation with one's employees is to be preferred over secrecy, along with a promise of help in securing alternative employment, should that be necessary. These actions respect the rights of employees. Boatright points out that one of the main views of an employee is that he or she is an *agent* of an employer, and as such is engaged to act in the interests of the employer. "Specifically, an employee as an agent has an obligation to work as directed, to protect confidential information, and above all, to be loyal."[7] Of course, an employee has the same obligation as a manager to act in an ethical manner.

Canadian J.-Robert Ouimet of Montreal is chairman of the board of a medium-sized company. He is well known in the business and political worlds of both Quebec and the rest of Canada for leading his company by following Christian principles. He has this to say about the responsibilities of an organization towards the people who work in the company:

The company must recognize that work exists for man and not man for work [the use of the masculine form is to be understood in the generic sense, that is, including men and women]; salaries and social benefits must be just, adequate, and at least comparable to those in other companies of similar size and activity; job enrichment must be seen to be as much a way of reducing the monotony of work as a way of contributing to people's moral and spiritual development, to their professional and technical competence, productivity, and efficiency; the company must encourage every activity that increases solidarity, brotherhood, compassion, human dignity, and people's development.[8]

As to the obligations of employees, Ouimet writes,

By their sustained efforts, all people working in the company have the primary duty of contributing to the constant and necessary growth of efficiency and productivity, for their own good, for that of their families, and for the common good.[9]

In conclusion, the dignity of each person is at the core of this commandment. Respect and honour naturally follow recognition of this truth, be it in a family setting, in civil society, in the corporate world, or in any social situation. Author Raymond Collins sums up the value of the human person in light of this commandment:

The fourth commandment ... indicates that human value lies in something other than human function. ... Might one not say that this commandment is based on a view which sees man's worth in his innate and God-related dignity rather than in his societal or functional value?[10]

By his incarnation, Jesus has raised our humanity to a new dignity. When we honour one another, we honour him.

5

The Fifth Commandment

You shall not kill.
—*Exodus* 20:13

I have been writing a monthly e-column on spirituality and ethics for over four years. One of the themes I have written about is the Ten Commandments. The piece I did on the fifth commandment received a flood of responses, all of them instructive, so I will begin this chapter with that issue.

We believe that human life is sacred, created as we are in the image and likeness of the Creator. God alone is the custodian of life. Issues such as abortion, euthanasia, suicide and capital punishment are the usual focus of this commandment, but what of the killing of the human spirit?

In an insightful article on the United States economy (this was around 2008–2010), writer Jeffrey Pfeffer notes that an overreliance on downsizing and layoffs was killing workers, the economy and even the bottom line.[1] First, he reflects on the previous two decades and points out that layoffs had become increasingly common in corporate life, in good times as well as bad. He acknowledges that there are circumstances in which a company has to downsize in order to survive. But he also draws on recent academic research, which finds that the costs of doing so when it is not a matter of company survival are often greater than the savings. There is the obvious toll on morale, the physical and health effects on employees, and the anxiety that infects remaining workers. In other words, there is a killing of the human spirit. Pfeffer writes:

> Layoffs literally kill people. In the United States, when you lose your job, you lose your health insurance, unless you can afford to temporarily maintain it under the pricey COBRA [Consolidated Omnibus Budget Reconciliation Act] provisions. Studies consistently show a connection between not having health insurance and individual mortality rates.[2]

In addition, when people lose their jobs, their sense of self-worth takes a serious hit – we put so much of our personal identity into our work. People get angry and depressed. In his article, Pfeffer notes that people who are angry and depressed and who believe they have been treated unfairly can lose psychological control and exact vengeance on those they deem responsible. Research shows that even people who have no history of violent behaviour are six times more likely to exhibit such behaviour after a layoff than similar people who remain employed.

Suicide rates also go up for those who have been fairly or unfairly dismissed. Such is the dramatic effect of losing one's job. Here is Pfeffer again: "Anyone who's suffered a layoff or watched a loved one lose a job can understand why downsizees exhibit increased rates of alcoholism, smoking, drug abuse, and depression."

In terms of the employment scene, living the fifth commandment in its fullness implies having a caring attitude towards those who have to be laid off in order for a company to survive. Pfeffer describes some compassionate ways to minimize the psychological damage of layoffs:

> Companies that behave humanely – by providing generous severance packages and allowing displaced employees to say goodbye to colleagues rather than marching them out the door – are likely to see a smaller hit to morale. Well-run companies also communicate clearly about why they're eliminating jobs....

Life is a precious gift entrusted to us by God. The fifth commandment includes respect for the dignity of each person – for their physical, emotional and mental health. We each have a responsibility to make sure our employment institutions safeguard life in all its forms.

Two of the respondents to my original article on this topic clearly confirm the insights of Pfeffer. One was in the banking business:

> My own experience was being fired from a finance firm by a person who was one of the most conniving, vindictive people I have ever met. What I discovered from this experience is that the after-effects of such an action stay with a person for the rest of his or her life. For me, it was good to leave this 'den of evil' where my boss absolutely sought to kill my spirit, but I still find myself lamenting the injustice of it all and the manner and basis for which I was let go. I have long ago forgiven my ex-boss – but not forgotten. I learned a lot about how not to treat others.

The other was an architect:

> I have had two separate conversations with fellow architects occasioned by your reflections on the fifth commandment. What you wrote goes to the heart of my own disquiet with business. I went to Mass the afternoon I read this and prayed for a better society, one that does not 'kill' in the cavalier fashion that many people in the business world call 'downsizing.' The survival of a company may be an issue, but at the core is treating business as a form of stewardship where people's lives are valued and respected.

Efforts to 'kill the human spirit' take various forms. Here are some other examples:

- Spousal abuse
- Parental abuse

- An abusive boss
- Stifling the creativity of others
- Sex trafficking and other kinds of enslavement
- Torture

Honour Human Life

The fifth commandment calls upon us to promote the physical, mental, emotional, spiritual and social well-being of each human person, including ourselves. Consequently, the commandment also forbids abortion, murder, euthanasia and any life-threatening acts. Pope John Paul II called the world to foster a "Culture of Life." In his encyclical letter *The Gospel of Life*, he enlisted our Blessed Mother to help us protect life in all its forms.

O Mary,
bright dawn of the new world,
Mother of the living,
to you do we entrust *the cause of life;*
Look down, O Mother,
upon the vast numbers
of babies not allowed to be born,
of the poor whose lives are made difficult,
of men and women
who are victims of brutal violence,
of the elderly and the sick killed
by indifference or out of misguided mercy.

Grant that all who believe in your Son
may *proclaim the Gospel of Life*
with honesty and love
to the people of our time.

Obtain for them the grace
to *accept that Gospel*
as a gift ever new,
the joy *of celebrating* it with gratitude

throughout their lives
and the courage to *bear witness to it*
resolutely, in order to build,
together with all people of good will,
the cultivation of truth and love,
to the praise and glory of God,
the Creator and lover of life.[3]

The call to promote a "Culture of Life" over the "Culture of Death" presents us with a number of challenges. Here are three, taken from The *United States Catholic Catechism for Adults*.[4] The first concerns relativism.

1. We need to counter the relativism that imperils human life, by recognizing that human freedom needs to be consistent with God's intentions and the laws that govern moral life.

Let's consider the subject of relativism and what it means. Professor of Moral Theology Rich Gula offers three schools of thought:

A. *Social relativists* look to what society approves in order to know what is morally right or wrong. For them, the moral and the customary are synonymous so that sociological studies are enough to confirm whether moral claims are true and reliable or not.

B. *Personal relativists* use the criterion of self-satisfaction to confirm what is right or wrong. "Do your own thing" is their familiar slogan. For them, the tools of psychology would be sufficient to determine whether a person is really satisfied or not.

C. The *emotivist school of relativism* claims, "The good is what I feel comfortable with." This school regards all moral evaluations as simply expressions of emotions, but not as statements which could be true or false.[5]

Fr. Gula goes on to conclude that ethical relativists such as these three will always be a seductive force as long as we live in a confusing world.

Santa Clara University Professor Manuel Velasquez points out that critics of ethical relativists argue that there are certain moral standards that the members of any society must accept if that society is to survive and if its members are to interact with each other effectively. Thus, all societies have norms: for example, against injuring or killing other members of the society.[6]

Why do some some people fall into relativism? Author Tom Morris suggests two main causes:

> First, relativism can serve as a very persuasive intellectual excuse for very bad behavior. If there is no absolute truth, there is no absolute moral truth, and we can get away with anything we want. Some people are relativists because it is a wonderful form of self-deception, licensing anything they want to do. Second, many academics have wanted to promote the virtue of tolerance in our pluralistic world, and have wrongly thought that relativism is the royal road to cultivating a firm and resilient openness to other people's beliefs.[7]

The second challenge around a culture of life versus a culture of death involves witnessing to God's presence:

2. We must witness God's providential presence to all creation and particularly to each human being. "Where God is denied, and people live as though he did not exist, or his commandments are not taken into account, the dignity of the human person and the inviolability of human life also end up being rejected or compromised."[8]

The third challenge relates to conscience:

3. We need to confront the weakening of conscience in modern society. Too many people fail to distinguish between good and evil when dealing with the value of human life. Moral

confusion leads many to support choices and policies that desecrate life.

Let us consider the meaning of our conscience from the point of view of the Second Vatican Council:

> In the depths of our conscience, we detect a law which does not impose, but which holds us to obedience. Always summoning us to love good and avoid evil, the voice of conscience when necessary speaks to our heart: do this, shun that. For we have in our heart a law written by God; to obey it is the very dignity of being human; according to it we will be judged (Romans 2:15-16). Conscience is the most secret core and sanctuary of a person. There we are alone with God, Whose voice echoes in our depths (John 1:3, 14).... Christians are joined with the rest of humanity in the search for truth, and for the genuine solution to the numerous problems which arise in the life of individuals from social relationships. Hence the more right conscience holds sway, the more persons and groups turn aside from blind choice and strive to be guided by the objective norms of morality.[9]

Back now to the *United States Catholic Catechism for Adults*:

> ... (moral) choices that were once considered criminal and immoral [like abortion and euthanasia—author] have become socially acceptable. Many consciences that were once formed by the Ten Commandments, Christ's moral teachings, and the Holy Spirit's Grace-filled guidance are now swayed by the moral confusion of the spirit of the times.[10]

How do we confront this issue?

• To counter relativism in all its forms, we need to make it clear in our teaching and preaching that there is such a reality as absolute truth and thus absolute moral truth. This teaching may take courage, at times, because we are bound to run into resistance. One slogan that will be thrown at us is that "we have to be politically correct." Which is nonsense. So ignore it. And continue telling the truth.

- We must be forthright in witnessing to our faith, not ashamed of our principles and values. Stephen Carter, in his masterful book, *Integrity*, writes, "the person truly living an integral life must be willing to say that he or she is acting consistently with what he or she has decided is right ... people of integrity are willing to tell us *why* they are doing what they are doing."[11] If 'doing' is so important, how much more so is witnessing with the spoken and written word. If we do not stand up for the truth, for the sanctity of human life, who will?

- We must do our best to help people understand the *why* of the Church's teaching on life issues, as expressed in the Ten Commandments and by stressing the dignity of the human person, made in the image and likeness of God. If a person is in ignorance about such teachings on a particular life issue and we become aware of this, we have a responsibility to present the Church's view in a brotherly or sisterly fashion so that his or her conscience will witness to the truth.

The hopeful result of these efforts is summed up in the *Catechism of the Catholic Church*: "The more a correct conscience prevails, the more do persons and groups turn aside from blind choice and try to be guided by objective standards of moral conduct" (CCC no. 1794).

A prayer that brings this chapter on respecting life in all its forms to a reflective conclusion is called "Respect for Life":

God of life and love,
you created us in your image
and sent your Son to bring us life.
Instill in us a respect for all life,
from conception to natural death.
Empower us to work for
justice for the poor.

Nourish us that we may
bring food to the hungry.
Inspire us to cherish
the fragile life of the unborn.
Strengthen us to bring comfort
to the chronically ill.
Teach us to treat the aging
with dignity and respect.
Bring us one day
into the glory of everlasting life.
We ask this
through Christ our Lord.
Amen.[12]

6

The Sixth and Ninth Commandments

You shall not commit adultery.
—*Exodus 20:14*

You shall not covet your neighbour's wife.
—*Exodus 20:17*

The Sixth Commandment

You shall not commit adultery.
—*Exodus 20:14*

A few years ago, the CEO of a medium-sized company hired me to give three 3-hour workshops on ethics to all of his employees: 100 people in all. At the beginning of each class, he introduced me and spoke frankly of his commitment to a workplace built on a strong moral foundation. He told his employees that the issue that most concerned him was inter-office romances. There are a lot of attractive single women in the company, while most of the men working there are married. He said further that inter-office romances would not be tolerated and were grounds for dismissal from the company.

There are a number of offenses against the dignity of marriage, but adultery shakes the very foundation of the marriage bond. In addition to the betrayal of one of the marriage partners by the other, there is the matter of justice. Here is what the *Catechism of the Catholic Church* has to say:

> Adultery is an injustice. The one who commits adultery fails in his [her] commitment. He [she] does injury to the sign of the covenant which the marriage bond is, transgresses the rights of the other spouse, and undermines the institution of marriage by breaking the contract on which it is based. He [she] compromises the good of human generation and the welfare of children who need their parents' stable union. (CCC no. 2381)

We have seen in previous chapters of this book that the commandments help us in our understanding both of God who is love and of what God wishes of us in our interpersonal relationships. This God lives in a mystery of loving communion. Professor of Moral Theology James F. Keenan points out that the moral code for the Israelite people was something naturally good for them. He writes: "… the law that God gave was a law not primarily for God's benefit and delight, but for ours. By the law, we could become freer and happier."[1] He continues, "Thomas Aquinas held that nothing bothered God about human conduct except when human beings brought harm to themselves…. Thomas believed that our well-being has always been the aim of the love and the wisdom of God."[2]

Adultery, or marital infidelity, brings harm not only to the spouse who is betrayed, but also to the betrayer, because this immoral act is an offense against the virtue of integrity. Integrity is about wholeness and unity; adultery is about selfishness and division. Adultery is a sin against love and against unity. Fidelity in marriage is built on mutual respect, mutual self-forgetfulness. "You shall not commit adultery" can also read "You shall not break the peace of a marriage!" points out Abd-ru-shin.[3] He continues, "Woe to the woman, woe to a man, be they young or old, who out of envy or flirtatiousness consciously brings discord or even strife between a couple!"[4]

The foundation of the marriage bond is love. In Ephesians 5:25-33, St. Paul compares love in marriage to the love Christ has for the Church. Fr. Pedro Arrupe, who was General Superior of the Society of Jesus (Jesuits) from 1965 to 1983, wrote a beautiful reflection on the power of love.

> Nothing is more practical than finding God,
> that is, than falling in love in a quite absolute,
> final way. What you are in love with,
> what seizes your imagination, will affect everything.
> It will decide what will get you out of bed in the morning,
> what you do with your evenings, how you will spend
> your weekends, what you read, who you know,
> what breaks your heart, and what amazes you with
> joy and gratitude.
> Fall in love, stay in love, and it will decide everything.[5]

Love and fidelity go hand in hand in a marriage. To deepen and further this reality, St. John Chrysostom suggests that young husbands should say to their wives:

> I have taken you in my arms and I love you, and I prefer you to my life itself … my most ardent dream is to spend it with you in such a way that we may be assured of not being separated in the life reserved for us … I place your love above all things, and nothing would be more bitter or painful to me than to be of a different mind than you. (CCC no. 2365)

The *Catechism of the Catholic Church*, in describing the sixth commandment, calls on spouses to practise permanent and exclusive fidelity to one another.[6] Emotional and sexual fidelity are essential to this commitment to the marriage covenant. The Creator established marriage as a reflection of his faithfulness to us. This is at the core of the integrity of the sacrament; adultery is a severe violation of this conjugal commitment. And not only adultery, but other threats as well, such as domestic violence. Married couples need the kind of foundation for their union that Fr. Arrupe describes and that St. John Chrysostom suggests in order to avoid temptation and stay true to their vows.

The sixth commandment encompasses the whole of human sexuality. Sexuality affects all aspects of the human person: mind, body and spirit. We each have a vocation to live chaste lives. About the virtue of chastity, we read in the *Catechism of the Catholic Church*: "Chastity means the successful integration of sexuality within the person and thus the inner unity of man [woman] in [their] bodily and spiritual being ... The virtue of chastity therefore involves the integrity of the person..." (CCC no. 2337).

A relatively new threat to an integrated sexuality is pornography. Pornography is the depiction of erotic behavior – as in pictures or videos – intended to cause sexual excitement. It objectifies people and is completely self-centred behaviour. Confessors and counsellors deal with this moral scourge frequently among their constituents. One friend of mine, who is a marriage counsellor, sees pornography as an epidemic. When someone comes to see me and it is clear that they are dealing with addictive behaviour as it relates to pornography and its usual 'partner' – masturbation – I recommend they seek counselling. I keep with me the names and contact information of two excellent counsellors in the city where I live. For the immediate present, I give the person a handout that features a helpful reflection from Daniel Spadaro, who is founder of Imago Dei Counseling:

> We are created with a desire to love and be loved. We long to be known, understood and accepted for who we are. Ultimately, God alone is capable of such perfect love and knowledge. Pornography, in contrast, distracts us from our call to love. When we are preoccupied with pornography, our mind and heart easily lose sight of what holds real value, including those who are close to us. Instead, we start to view others through a lens of self-gratification. No one intends to trade his or her need for real love with a cheap thrill. It subtly slips away as one becomes distracted and disconnected from self, others, and the reality that one's mind and heart are changing. When someone is hooked on pornography he or she can lose the ability to be captivated by love.[7]

Also on the handout is a prayer for divine assistance when temptations to sexual addictive behaviour appear:

Deliver me, Lord, from every evil,
from temptation and the occasion of sin.
Graciously grant peace in my soul, that
by the help of your mercy
I may honor my body, my mind, and my heart.
Help me to promote balance in my life,
Balance of prayer, exercise, and quality time with friends.
Constantly call me to new life
now and forever. Amen.

Jesuit spiritual counsellor Fr. Jim Hanley, who ministers to both priests and laypeople, emphasizes the need, especially for those in ministry, to seek balance in their lives. He writes,

One of the strategies of the evil spirit is to throw our life out of balance. We feel pressured to keep up with all the things in our life and lose our sense of priorities. We think that we can put all our time and effort into some project and then have time to rest and pray when we finish. However, often we find that there is another project or activity that presses upon us when we finish the first one.

Fr. Hanley suggests to priests that they can lose their sense of intimacy with God and endanger their relationships with others if they are out of balance. He suggests spending some quality time reflecting on how balanced their life is and how much time they spend on each of the following every week (this applies also to laypeople):

- Sufficient sleep
- Diet
- Exercise
- Time with fellow priests (I would add, and with significant lay friends; for laypeople, I would say significant peers)
- Recreation

- Quality prayer each day
- Spiritual reading
- Spiritual direction on a regular basis

The primary goal of our life is to grow in intimacy with God. At various times, this may be more with the Father or the Son or the Holy Spirit. Prayer enables this to happen. Living a balanced life is the best guarantee that we will be faithful to prayer and thus grow daily in our friendship with God.

The Ninth Commandment

You shall not covet your neighbour's wife.
—*Exodus 20:17*

Covetousness is the inordinate desire for something that is not yours, that belongs to someone else. There are three kinds of covetousness: lust of the flesh, lust of the eyes, and pride of life. St. Paul treats this as a struggle between the spirit and the flesh:

> My brothers (and sisters), remember you have been called to live in freedom – but not a freedom that gives free reign to the flesh … My point is that you should live in accord with the spirit and you will not yield to the cravings of the flesh. The flesh lusts against the spirit and the spirit against the flesh. (Galatians 5:13, 16-17)

St. John continues this theme, writing of "carnal allurements," which are a disordered desire for sensuality (1 John 2:16). Disordered desire comes in many forms. One of its tragic present-day forms is sex trafficking. Sex trafficking reaches every corner of the globe. It is a clear deviation from the ninth commandment, because it preys on other people's daughters. The trafficking of human beings involves the use of fraud, force and coercion for the purpose of forced prostitution.

According to the Polaris Project, a United States organization fighting against all forms of human trafficking, including slave labour, sex traffickers frequently target vulnerable people with histories of abuse and then use violence, threats, lies, false promises, debt bondage or other forms of control and manipulation to keep victims involved in the sex industry.[8] Sex trafficking occurs in a wide variety of venues of the overall sex industry, but also in hotels, motels and truck stops. Those involved in the crime of sex trafficking and those who participate in any way, which includes pornography (adult and child), are in grave moral danger.

How to avoid the pitfalls of lust of the flesh and lust of the eyes? The *Catechism of the Catholic Church* offers the following reflections under the title "Purification of the Heart":

> The heart is the seat of moral personality. The struggle against carnal covetousness entails purifying the heart and practicing temperance. (CCC no. 2517)

> The ninth commandment is directly connected to the sixth Beatitude: "Blessed are the pure in heart, for they shall see God" (Matthew 5:8). "Pure in heart" refers to those who have attuned their intellects and wills to the demands of God's holiness. (CCC no. 2518)

> It enables us to perceive the human body – ours and our neighbour's (male or female) – as a temple of the Holy Spirit. (CCC no. 2519)

In the battle for purity, and it is a battle, in my experience, we need to practise a number of virtues, but above all we need to be faithful to prayer, as St. Paul reminds us:

> Draw your strength from the Lord and his mighty power. Put on the armour of God so that you may be able to stand firm against the tactics of the devil. Our battle is not against human forces but against the principalities and powers, the rulers of the world of darkness, the evil spirits in the region above.... (Ephesians 6:10-17)

In our struggle against concupiscence (lust) of the flesh and disordered desires such as coveting another person's spouse, the following actions can help us.

- Practising the virtue of *chastity*, for chastity enables us to live with an undivided heart. Chastity applies to single, married and celibate alike, each according to their state in life.
- Having *purity of intention*, which consists of seeking our true end by doing what God asks of us according to the Ten Commandments and other church teachings.
- Practising *purity of vision*, or 'modesty of the eyes,' as the Jesuits taught me. A businessman friend and I were in conversation one day on the reality of today's fashion for women. He, a happily married man, and I, a committed celibate, were wondering how best to deal with the physical attractiveness of what we were seeing on a daily basis. We came up with a mantra that works for us: "Look, but don't stare!"
- Maintaining a certain *modesty*, which is an integral part of temperance. Modesty, according to the *Catechism of the Catholic Church*, "protects the intimate center of the person. It means refusing to unveil what should remain hidden. It guides how one looks at others and behaves towards them in conformity with the dignity of persons" (CCC no. 2521). "Modesty involves practicing decency; it protects the mystery of human beings and their love" (CCC no. 2522).
- Teaching *modesty* to children and teens by emphasizing the dignity of our humanity, created as we are by a loving God and in God's image. This means helping our young people to have the wisdom and the discipline to ignore and avoid sexually suggestive ads, R-rated movies and websites that show inappropriate sexual content.

Taking on the prevailing social climate when it threatens the moral fabric of society takes courage – moral courage. I would suggest six 'movements' of this kind of courage:

1. The courage to *acknowledge* the reality of moral permissiveness in the city where you live, in whatever forms it takes.

2. The courage to listen to the stories of those who have been personally affected by the scourge of sex trafficking – both victims and parents.

3. The courage to develop an informed conscience and listen to it.

4. The humility to ask God for the courage to do something to combat threats to the moral fabric of your community and to join with others of like mind in this effort on both the local and the regional level.

5. The courage of commitment, of staying the course for the long haul with patient endurance.

6. The courage to witness, by personal example, to the values of the gospel and to the sacredness of human life, especially in relation to the sixth and ninth commandments.

To conclude this chapter on the sixth and ninth commandments, here are two quotes for reflection. The first appeared earlier in the chapter, but bears repeating.

St. John Chrysostom suggests that young husbands should say to their wives: I have taken you in my arms, and I love you, and I prefer you to my life itself. For the present life is nothing, and my most ardent dream is to spend it with you in such a way that we may be assured of not being separated in the life reserved for us ... I place your love above all things, and nothing would be more bitter or painful to me than to be of a different mind than you. (CCC no. 2365)

I thought that continence (self-restraint) arose from one's own powers, which I did not recognize in myself. I was foolish enough not to know ... that no one can be continent unless you grant it. For you would surely have granted it if my inner groaning had reached your ears and I with firm faith had cast my cares on you. (CCC no. 2520; the quote is from St. Augustine, *Confessions*, ch. 6)

7

The Seventh Commandment

You shall not steal.
—*Exodus* 20:15

The seventh commandment can be summed up in three words: honesty, respect and responsibility. *Honesty* involves being truthful and trustworthy; people who are honest do not lie, cheat or steal. We are to *respect* the rights of all people to material goods and take *responsibility* for the stewardship of these goods.

Honesty

My parents had a strong commitment to the virtue of honesty. I learned this the hard way, but I learned it well. How well became clear in my first job after graduating from college with a degree in marketing. The company I went to work for assigned me to a sales territory that involved some travelling. Whenever I came back from a trip, I would dutifully and accurately write down my expenses and hand them in to the company treasurer (what the CFO, or Chief Financial Officer, was known as in those days).

One day, one of the older salesmen came to my office with a complaint. "You are making us look bad. You are too honest!" he said, adding that the cause of his concern was the way I reported my expenses. His remark made it clear that he and some of the other salesmen were padding their expense accounts. This had become obvious to the treasurer when he compared what I was spending with what they were spending. This was a moment of truth for me. Should I give in to his request to pad my accounting in order to be one of the guys, or stay true to my desire to be an honest person? Fortunately, I had also learned about courage from my mother and father, and so nicely but firmly I told the salesman that I was not going to change. There was some tension in the office for a while, but eventually things died down and I was accepted.

Padding an expense account is one way we go against the seventh commandment, because this is a form of stealing – stealing from the company where we work. This commandment, according to the *Catechism of the Catholic Church*, "forbids unjustly taking or keeping the goods of one's neighbor and wronging him [her] in any way with respect to [their] goods" (CCC no. 2401). "In matters of economics, this form of stealing also relates to the virtue of justice: respect for human dignity means preserving our neighbour's rights and rendering to him [her] what is [their] due" (CCC no. 2407).

Let's look further at stealing in the workplace. The following examples come to mind.

- Using company time to check and respond to personal e-mails.
- Not doing an honest day's work for the pay you agreed to.
- Taking items from the office or other job locales without asking.
- Cheating on a test. This is something that has affected some branches of the US military, as well as organizations in the private sector.
- Falsifying a resumé. This is hiding the truth from those who have a right to know it.
- Engaging in insider trading, which is stealing possible monetary gain from another by your foreknowledge.
- Cooking the books – when a company falsifies financial statements to make things look better than they are. Prime

examples of this activity are Enron (2001) and World Com (2002). This is stealing the truth from shareholders, investors, regulators and the general public.

Professor of Business Ethics Marianne Jennings, in her insightful book *The Seven Signs of Ethical Collapse*, reflects on the business scandals of 2001 to 2003. First, she makes the point that the MBA curriculum, at least in the US, of the 1980s and 1990s taught the tools of managing earnings without discussing the ethical issues involved in manipulating them. She writes:

> These executives were trained by a curriculum that convinced its charges that they were better, smarter, and above the proletarian notion of reporting debt and expenses. Managing earnings was taught as a means of delivering shareholder value. It wasn't cooking the books, it was "financial engineering" ... Skill was everything. Values were nothing. There were no moral absolutes.[1]

On the subject of cheating, Kirk O. Hanson, who is Executive Director of the Markkula Center for Applied Ethics at Santa Clara University, lists four reasons why people cheat in the corporate world.

- Some people are driven by ambition and will use any means to get ahead.
- Some fear the embarrassment of failure.
- Some do so because they think everybody else cheats – "you have to cheat to be competitive," they say.
- An increasing number of cheaters argue that they must cheat to resist what they consider 'unfair' new systems of accountability.[2]

I want to return for a moment to my family. My father was a natural born salesman, and he passed this gift on to me. He helped me to see some of the ways a salesperson could go against the seventh commandment – by exaggerating the value of the product, which also goes by the name of 'false advertising'; unfair and untrue comments about the character of one's competitors in order to make the sale, which is robbing another of their good reputation through slander; and taking advantage of people who are vulnerable to smooth sales pitches for one's own personal gain. Above all, he advocated being honest and treating each person you work with respectfully.

We honour the spirit of the seventh commandment when we

- Give credit where credit is due, and do not claim someone else's ideas as our own.
- Pay a just and living wage.
- Pay our taxes.
- Promote and implement safety in the workplace; not to do so is to risk stealing the good health of employees.
- Protect proprietary information.
- If in the casino business, take responsibility beyond the obligatory posted "800" phone number for the problem gambler to make sure his or her livelihood is not threatened by their addictive behaviour. We need to be like the responsible bartender who refuses to sell another drink to someone who has to drive home or who calls a taxi for this person, if necessary.[3]

St. Paul points us in the right ethical direction for this commandment:

See to it, then, that you put an end to lying; let everyone speak the truth to his neighbour, for we are members of one another.... The man who has been stealing must steal no longer; rather let him work with his hands at honest labour so that he will have something to share with those in need. Never let evil talk pass your lips; say only the good things people need to hear, things that will really help them. (Ephesians 4:25-29)

Respect

Catholics are called to promote the common good. This means not only caring for those who are physically near to us, but the whole human family. The seventh commandment requires us to respect the rights of all people to material goods. The Second Vatican Council expressed it this way:

> Every social group must take account of the needs and legitimate aspirations of other groups, and even of the general welfare of the entire human family.
>
> ... There must be made available to all people everything necessary for leading a life truly human, such as food, clothing, and shelter; the right to choose a state of life freely and to found a family; the right to education, to employment, to a good reputation, to respect, to appropriate information, to activity in accord with the upright norm of one's conscience, to protection of privacy and to rightful freedom in matters religious too.[4]

Respect for people and their goods requires the practice of three virtues in particular: *temperance, justice* and *solidarity*. *Temperance* allows us to moderate our attachment to this world's goods. The question "How much is enough for one person?" comes to mind here. *Justice* preserves our neighbour's rights and renders him or her what is their due. *Solidarity* means following the Golden Rule – "In everything do to others, as you would have them do to you" is the Christian version (Matthew 7:12). Every major world religion has a variation on this theme.[5]

When it comes to the virtue of *justice* and its connection to the seventh commandment, we need go no further than the following words of Pope Francis: "Money must serve, not rule! The Pope loves everyone, rich and poor alike, but he is obliged in the name of Christ to remind all that the rich must help, respect, and promote the poor."[6]

Then he quotes St. John Chrysostom: "Not to share one's wealth with the poor is to steal from them and to take away their livelihood. It is not our own goods which we hold, but theirs."[7]

I learned the lesson about compassion for the poor from my mother. Although she came from a wealthy family, her heart was filled with concern for those in our parish who had less than we did. I can remember times when, after I got home from elementary school, she would enlist my help in bringing canned goods and other needed food items to families, to Sisters at a nearby cloistered convent who depended on others for their basic needs, and to a parish other than our own with many low-income parishioners. Because my father was in the food business, he would bring home samples that, in his mind, were for our family. When he would find the cupboard where we stored these items bare, he knew we could not have eaten all that was there. He was a formidable character so, in addition to being inspired by my mother to be a person of compassion, I was also in awe of her courage in standing up to my father as she patiently explained to him where the food had gone.

I have drawn from the lesson about compassion that I learned from my mother over the past 50 years, as I lived among and served African American people; in Tijuana, Mexico; on a Blackfoot First Nations Reserve in southern Alberta; among Mexican-American people in Las Vegas; and for a summer in Calcutta, India.

This experience of learning from my mother's actions as well as her words brings up the important point of early character building. Without explicitly mentioning the words "common good," her example taught me volumes about this value. While my father emphasized the importance of honesty, my mother stressed doing something very practical to make the lives of others better.

When you think back on your own history, who taught you to be honest and to value the idea of treating each person with respect?

Responsibility

This characteristic refers to the future, to the generations that will come after us. We have a responsibility to them to make sure that the integrity of creation is safe. Not to do so is to steal from them.

This calls for a commitment to what is known as sustainability, and its corollary, sustainable development.[8]

Sustainable development implies the achievement of continued economic and social development without detriment to the environment and the earth's natural resources. Sustainability is viewed as a long-term evolutionary commitment. In the corporate world, companies are encouraged to aim continuously to reduce their consumption of natural resources and to develop new products, services and processes that will help their organization, and industry, to achieve sustainable goals.

Reflecting on the universal need for such a view, the *Catechism of the Catholic Church* states: "The seventh commandment forbids unjustly taking or keeping the goods of one's neighbor and wronging him [her] in any way with respect to [their] goods.... The goods of creation are destined for the whole human race" (CCC nos. 2401–2402).

The "whole human race," of course, does not just refer to those living now, but to all who will ever live!

Sustainable actions would include water conservation (I am particularly aware of this because I live in the desert, where we and four other states are dependent on one river, the Colorado); reducing greenhouse gas emissions; increasing solar power and wind energy; cutting back on deforestation and sponsoring tree planting initiatives; and so forth. Keeping corporations and governments accountable for 'green' commitments is also necessary. In order to honour the environment in the long-term, we need to

- Say "No" to a philosophy of indifference to what happens to our planet.
- Expand our sense of the common good to include future generations.
- Help developing countries to do their part in this endeavour.

- Openly and courageously face threats to the integrity of creation regardless of whether the threats are from natural climate changes or the folly of humans.

If we think, "But I am only one person. What possible effect could my actions (like recycling) have?" we need to be reminded of something Christine Todd Whitman, former Administrator of the US Environmental Protection Agency, noted: "Anyone who thinks they are too small to make a difference has never tried to fall asleep with a mosquito in the room."

Pope Francis adds a theological slant to having confidence in our efforts to make a difference. Here he reflects on our role in helping Christ to build the kingdom of God:

> The kingdom is here, it returns, it struggles to flourish anew. Christ's resurrection everywhere calls forth seeds of that new world; even if they are cut back, they grow again, for the resurrection is already secretly woven into the fabric of this history, for Jesus did not rise in vain.
>
> Because we do not always see these seeds growing, we need an interior certainty, a conviction that God is able to act in every situation, even amid apparent setbacks: 'we have this treasure in earthen vessels' (II Corinthians 4:7). This certainty is often called 'a sense of mystery.' It involves knowing with certitude that all those who entrust themselves to God in love will bear fruit.... We can be sure that none of our acts of love will be lost, nor any of our acts of sincere concern for others. No single act of love for God will be lost, no generous effort is meaningless, no painful endurance is wasted.[9]

Honesty, respect and responsibility protect and promote the integrity of the seventh commandment. Each, we have seen, relates to stealing – be it another's goods, reputation or the legacy of future generations.

8

The Eighth Commandment

You shall not bear false witness against your neighbour.
—*Exodus 20:16*

The eighth commandment is about truth: living in it, avoiding misrepresenting it in our interpersonal relationships, bearing witness to it and protecting it. This moral principle flows from the Bible teaching that God the Creator is the source of truth.

In the Hebrew Scriptures, we find these words:

Your word, O Lord, endures forever; it is firm as the heavens.
Through all generations your truth endures;
you have established the earth, and it stands firm.
(Psalm 119:89-90)

In Jesus, the whole of God's truth is made manifest. St. John makes this clear in his Gospel. When the apostle Thomas asked Jesus about his own direction in life, Jesus told him: "I am the way, and the truth, and the life; no one comes to the Father except through me" (14:5-7).

When Jesus faced Pilate, Pilate asked him if he were a king. Jesus responded: "It is you who say I am a king. The reason I was born, the reason why I came into the world, is to testify to the truth. Anyone committed to the truth hears my voice" (John 18:37).

And what is the core of this truth? Again, we go to John's Gospel: "God so loved the world that he gave his only Son, that whoever believes in him may not die but may have eternal life" (3:16).

"May not die" – in the darkness of sin and un-freedom. Jesus said to those Jewish people who had come to believe in him, "If you live according to my teaching, you are truly my disciples; then you will know the truth and the truth will set you free" (John 8:31-32). Free to do what? To live the commandments and the spirit of the Beatitudes. Jesus goes on to tell us that the Spirit of truth – the Holy Spirit – guides us to all truth (John 16:13).

Human beings by nature tend towards the truth. Cicero, the ancient Roman philosopher, wrote, "Nature has instilled in our minds an insatiable desire to see truth."[1] From the Roman Catholic point of view, we read in the Second Vatican Council's Declaration on Religious Freedom that

> It is in accordance with their dignity as persons – that is, beings endowed with reason and free will and therefore privileged to bear personal responsibility – that all men and women are both impelled by nature and bound by a moral obligation to seek the truth, especially religious truth. They are also bound to adhere to the truth once they come to know it....[2]

Living in the truth, then, means to constantly seek it. A story from the New Testament that bears this out concerns the two disciples returning to their hometown of Emmaus after Jesus' death. They go from a firm belief in him as the Chosen One of God to being so disheartened by what happened to him that they are having doubts about the truth they thought they knew. Then along comes a stranger. He proceeds to show them why the Christ had to suffer; he leads them through the words of the prophets. Their spirits are so lifted by this explanation that they invite the stranger to dine with them. At table with him, it all comes together for them; they recover the truth of their faith.

"Stay with us, for it is nearly evening and the day is almost over" [they say to the stranger]. So he went in to stay with them. And it happened that, while he was with them at table, he took bread, said the blessing, broke it, and gave it to them. With that their eyes were opened and they recognized him. (Luke 24:13-35)

We will continue with some more general comments about truth later in the chapter.

Offenses Against Truth in Our Interpersonal Relationships

"You shall love the Lord your God
with your whole heart, with your whole soul,
and with all your mind.
You shall love your neighbour as yourself."
(Matthew 21:37-38)

Here we find the two basic truths of our Christian faith. The first part refers to the first three commandments; the other seven refer to loving our neighbour as ourselves. We find an echo in the Psalms:

O Lord, who shall sojourn in your tent?
Who shall dwell on your holy mountain?
He who walks blamelessly and does justice;
who thinks the truth in his heart
and slanders not with his tongue;
who harms not his fellow man,
nor takes up a reproach against his neighbour. (Psalm 15:1-3)

And how might we harm others by our tongue, by an evil deed, or even by silence? Here are some examples:

- By rashly judging others.
- By gossiping.
- By detraction: the unjust telling of someone else's faults.[3]

- By calumny: remarks contrary to the truth, which harms the reputation of others and gives occasion for false judgments concerning them. (CCC no. 2477)

When someone shares with me that they have a problem with one of the above, I give them a prayer written by Eusebius of Caesarea (c. 263–339 AD), a bishop and historian in the early Church:

May I be no one's enemy, and may I be the friend of that which is eternal and abides.
May I love, seek, and attain only that which is good.
May I wish for all people's happiness and envy none.
May I never rejoice in the ill-fortune of one who has wronged me.
May I win no victory that harms either me or my opponent.
May I respect myself. May I always tame that which rages within me.
May I never discuss who is wicked and what wicked things they have done,
know good people and follow in their footsteps.[4]

To continue the litany of offenses against truth in our interpersonal relationships, here are some other examples:

- Misrepresenting the truth: for example, by false accusation fuelled by jealousy, resentment, rage, hatred or just plain vindictiveness.
- Libel, which is a published false statement that is damaging to a person's or an organization's reputation. Libel is connected to slander.
- Framing someone for a crime they did not commit.
- Perjury: the offense of willfully telling an untruth, in a court, after having taken an oath. (CCC no. 2476)

Living as we do in a digital age, we can find new forms of distorting the truth on the Internet. Perhaps you have been affected by the following, or know someone who has:

- Cyberbullying. According to stopbullying.gov, this form of distorting the truth and causing harm, especially to young people, takes place using electronic technology such as cellphones, computers and tablets, as well as social media sites, text messages, chat and websites. Mean-spirited texts or emails, embarrassing photos and videos, and false profiles are some examples of this offense against the truth. Cyber-bullying can happen 24 hours a day, 7 days a week, and can reach a kid even when he or she is alone. The damaging messages can be posted anonymously and distributed quickly to a very wide audience.[5]

Behind each item in our litany, of course, is one main vice: lying. Before we consider this moral scourge, it is important to look at some antidotes to false witnessing.

In the *Catechism of the Catholic Church*, about the eighth commandment, we read: "Christ's disciples have 'put on the new man, created after the likeness of God in true righteousness and holiness.' By 'putting away falsehood,' they are to 'put away all malice and all guile and insincerity and envy and all slander'" (CCC no. 2475).

This quote is inspired by St. Paul, who writes:

> … you must lay aside your former way of life and the old self which deteriorates through illusion and desire, and acquire a fresh, spiritual way of thinking. You must put on that new [person] created in God's image, whose justice and holiness are born of truth. (Ephesians 4:22-24)

I have been fascinated with this passage from Paul for a long time, ever since I read about Thomas Merton's description of the true self and the false self.[6] According to Merton, the true self is the self in Christ grounded in the love of God. This is that part of me that really believes I am loved unconditionally by God and, therefore, wants to do what God wants – out of love. The false self is that part of me that does not believe in God's personal and everlasting love and therefore wants to exist outside of the reach of God's will. The false self exposes itself whenever we choose to go against one of the commandments. In the case of the eighth commandment, the false self chooses the opposite of truth in one or more of its many forms.

The only way I can become my true self is through the death of the false self. My incomplete self must die for the true self to rise. We work together with God in this dynamic process. Allow me to illustrate this point with a story from my own life.

One of the many benefits of living in a religious community is that we rub shoulders with a great variety of people of all ages, each with our own personalities and peculiarities. Somewhere along the way, I discovered one of the aspects of my false self. I learned, through trial and error, that if someone in the community did (or said) something that bothered me, I had to go and talk with the person as soon as possible – if I was really annoyed, after I got past my anger – or else the "ant hill" of the annoyance would very soon become a "mountain" between us. I often had to face a fear as well: usually, the fear of rejection. When I was able to overcome the fear, though, not only would the relationship be saved, but also my sense of self would improve.

Bearing Witness to the Truth

"Truth stands outside the doors of our souls ... and knocks," wrote Gregory of Nyssa (335–395 AD), a bishop and erudite theologian who made significant contributions to the doctrine of the Trinity and the Nicene Creed. The key is to open that door and let truth in. It takes courage to do this, to

- Face the truth, no matter how personally challenging it may be.
- Live it consistently.
- Say openly why you believe what you do, even when it is an unpopular stance.

I discovered this reality a number of years ago, when I was invited by the Conference of Religious Women of South Africa to come and give talks on the social mission of the Church.[7] This was before apartheid ended. I gladly accepted, not fully realizing at first the danger that lay ahead. It was against the law in South Africa at that time to speak about social justice for African people, yet that is what the social mission of the Church calls us to do: speak out about injustice. As I prepared for the trip, the Sisters sent me articles to read. Some of the papers were devastating in their description of the evils of the apartheid system. I started getting nervous when one Sister told me to expect government informants at my talks. The first conference I gave, a two-day event, was in Johannesburg. There were about a hundred Sisters in attendance – some from South Africa and some missionary Sisters from a variety of European countries.

The Sisters in charge of the workshop decided that they would circulate among the other participants on the opening day to get their reaction to my talks. On the first day, I presented the fundamental principles of the social mission of the church. That evening, the team and I met. One Sister said that the Sisters she had spoken with liked what I had offered, but would like me, on the second day, to talk more explicitly about the evils of apartheid. Another said that there was a woman in attendance who was not a Sister: a government informant! That evening, I sat in my room, thinking about what to present the following day. Fear gripped me. "What if the informant returns?" I asked myself. "I could get into real trouble, even end up in jail." The truth of the evils inherent in apartheid was right in front of me. I asked the Holy Spirit for some extra courage. And then, inspired by the Spirit, I wrote a scathing critique of the apartheid system, even bringing in the devil as one instigator of it.

The next morning I stood at the podium, adrenaline pumping, knees knocking, and gave the talk exactly as I had written it the night before. In the discussion following the talk, one of the Sisters stood up and said that she had been struggling to find God in her ministry because of the injustices she saw daily. And then she said, "I felt the presence of God as I listened to your talk this morning!" For me, hearing those words was worth the whole trip.

There was no informant at the morning talk, but I did not find this out until after I gave my critique of the system of apartheid. Still, the experience of doing that presentation emboldened me for the rest of the talks I gave on the trip.

Bearing witness to the truth basically means saying "No" to lying. Lying is an intentional misstatement of the truth.[8] The *Catechism of the Catholic Church* says, "A lie consists in speaking a falsehood with the intention of deceiving" (CCC no. 2482). In our personal life, one problem with lying, according to my friend and Las Vegas attorney John F. O'Reilly, is that it severely injures our reputation and our credibility, which in turn damages the other person's ability to trust us. All relationships are founded on mutual trust. This idea is explained in detail in *Theology for Teachers*: "If we cannot normally expect people to tell the truth, if we constantly suspect that they may be lying, then we cannot trust them, and cannot really communicate with them."[9] Lying is a 'lose-lose-lose' situation, because all the parties involved are harmed, including the liar. It is an assault on human dignity. When caught in a lie, people will do the darnedest things to wiggle out of it, reports James Lamb, a businessman in Las Vegas: "They will say things like, 'I didn't mean to say it like that,' or 'That's not what I meant,' or 'You misunderstood me,' or 'That wasn't the meaning of the word I used,' and so forth."

When reflecting on the truth and the importance of truth-telling, it is also important to recognize that the right to communication of the truth is not unconditional (CCC no. 2488). In our commitment to fraternal love, we are required in certain situations to discern whether it is appropriate to reveal the truth to someone who asks for it. Here is what the Catholic Church teaches about this point:

> Charity and respect for the truth should dictate the response to every request for information or communication. The good and safety of others, respect for privacy, and the common good are sufficient reasons for being silent about what ought not

be known or for making use of a discreet language. The duty to avoid scandal often commands strict discretion. No one is bound to reveal the truth to someone who does not have the right to know it. (CCC no. 2489)

The secret of the sacrament of reconciliation is a prime example. Professional secrets, confidential information and the like should also be preserved with confidentiality unless there is a grave reason for divulging the information.

This brings us back to protecting personal privacy, whether in the mass media, on social media or in everyday conversation. Jesus summed up the eighth commandment in a short but profound statement: "Love your neighbour as yourself" (Matthew 22:39).[10]

9

The Tenth Commandment

You shall not covet ... anything that is your neighbour's ...
You shall not desire your neighbour's house ...
nor anything else that belongs to him.
—*Exodus 20:17*

The tenth commandment complements the ninth, which is concerned with not coveting another person's spouse. It also connects to the seventh commandment, which prohibits stealing. The *Catechism of the Catholic Church* points out that the tenth commandment concerns the intentions of the heart (CCC no. 2534). Jesus refers to this dynamic in Matthew's Gospel: "Where your treasure is, there will your heart be also" (6:21).

Coveting the goods of others is at the root of most of the financial scandals of the last 20 years. Covetousness ultimately leads to the unjust acquisition of what a person covets. Hence the vices of greed and avarice, jealousy and envy are directly linked to this distortion of the heart. When our desires exceed the limits of reason, we are tempted to commit various kinds of fraud – bank, mortgage or wire, embezzlement, tax evasion, and so on.

Greed is the desire to accumulate material goods without limit. However, this is a fool's quest, because one who loves money will never have money enough. Hank Shea, a former federal prosecutor of those convicted of white-collar crimes, shares his thoughts on this theme, and gives two examples of this truth:

Learn to be satisfied with what you have legitimately earned. Greed is a vicious vice that can destroy you.

While this may sound trite, it is important. If you judge success in life by what you can accumulate, you will never be content – someone will always have more, your children or others will always want more from you, and therefore, you will never have enough.

Among the many former lawyers whom I prosecuted, two examples stand out. One was legitimately earning more than $ 1 million a year as a personal injury attorney and the other was serving as an elected official and making a decent living as a lawyer. However, this wasn't enough for either of them; instead, they stole from vulnerable clients. Now they have lost everything – their freedom, their livelihood, their marriages, and their self-respect and reputations.[1]

Envy, like greed, is a capital sin. Envy refers to the sadness at the sight of another's goods. Consider the following story from the Hebrew scriptures.

Ahab was the King of Samaria. There was a vineyard next to his palace owned by a man named Naboth. Ahab wanted to acquire Naboth's land and make it his vegetable garden. When Naboth refused to give up his ancestral heritage, Ahab's reaction was to go into a major funk – "Lying down on his bed, he turned away from food and would not eat" (1 Kings 21:4). When his wife, Jezebel, discovered the reason for Ahab's meltdown, she took the matter into her own devious hands, fulfilling another aspect of envy – the immoderate desire to acquire another's goods for oneself, even by unjust means. She cooked up a scheme to falsely accuse Naboth of a crime that was punishable by death from stoning. Upon his death, she handed over the deed to her husband, who without hesitation got up and went to take possession of Naboth's land.

This sad story of envy and violence led Ambrose of Milan (340–397 AD) to exclaim: "Ahab is not one person, someone born long ago: every day, alas, the world sees Ahabs reborn, never to die out ... Neither is Naboth one person, a poor man once murdered: every day some Naboth is done to death, every day the poor are murdered."[2]

Just so in our own day.

Las Vegas attorney Michael E. Buckley shared with me the following modern spin on the problem: "It is common to hear, 'If I only had this or that material possession, everything in my life would be better.' We can get stuck in this mindset especially if we feel we have been dealt a 'short hand' in life while others haven't."

Implicit in Mr. Buckley's reflection are two basic human questions: What gives my life meaning? What is the ultimate source of my personal identity?

I asked a number of friends to reflect on the topic of coveting another's goods. Their responses touch directly on these two life questions.

Bob Brown, former publisher of the *Las Vegas Review Journal* and now President of Opportunity Village in Las Vegas, shared the following:

> Greed, envy and the inordinate desire for material things are the world's most insidious dispositions. We are an unhappy people. We want and want and want even more. This desire leaves us unfulfilled and feeling empty inside. The new car loses its new car smell; the newest trendy clothes wear out. Advertisers keep us focused on the latest fashions as symbols of the 'good life,' which leaves those who are economically poor feeling inadequate. The fog that consumerism creates is relentless.[3]

Canadian educators Heather Jamieson and Sandy Gillis add an Alberta viewpoint:

> Our current culture – especially the marketing ads that shape it and our values – encourages us to covet what our neighbours

have. We are constantly told that we do not have enough, that more/bigger/better are to be preferred, and that the measure of who we are is what we possess. What one does for a living is seen as having more value the greater the job title and the amount of one's salary; this leaves many people feeling inadequate. This in turn easily leads those who have less to envy those who have more. Basically, we are being sold a 'bill of goods' as to what makes us truly happy.

Las Vegan Jeannie Hamrick agrees that we have been duped by the culture: "'This product will make you a better person' feeds our desire for status. It is an illusion; 'if you do not possess it, you are a failure' is also false."[4]

Commenting on Jesus' message that "Where your treasure is, there will your heart be also" (Matthew 6:21), Dominican Sister Janet Ackerman suggests we need to change our mindset from 'covet' to 'treasure.' "When we covet, we are unable to be thankful for what we have, unable to find value in it."

Some Aids to Combating Covetnousness

Having a 'poverty of spirit' is the best disposition to directly contradict the desire to covet. It is the first of Jesus' eight Beatitudes: "Blessed are the poor in spirit; the reign of God is theirs" (Matthew 5:3). The Beatitudes are Jesus' mission statement. They reveal an order of happiness and grace, gratitude for what we have and generosity of heart. 'Poverty of spirit' means having a healthy detachment from all created goods – or as Buddhism puts it, 'engaged non-attachment.'[5]

In Chapter 1 of this book we considered the first meditation in the Spiritual Exercises of St. Ignatius of Loyola, "Principle and Foundation." We did this in relation to avoiding making idols of any created thing, honouring these instead of God. Here, we revisit this meditation in relation to the temptation to covet what others have.

After answering one of life's basic questions – What gives my life meaning? "To live with God forever" – Ignatius reminds us that all is gift, given to us so we can know God more easily and return God's love more readily.

Here are the pertinent sections in the meditation for having a positive detachment from earthly goods:

> We appreciate and use all these gifts of God insofar as they help us develop as loving persons. But if any of these gifts become the center of our lives, they displace God and so hinder our growth towards our goal.

> In everyday life, then, we must hold ourselves in balance before all these created gifts.... We should not fix our desires on health or sickness, wealth or poverty, success or failure, a long life or a short one. For everything has the potential of calling forth in us a deeper response to our life in God.[6]

St. Paul is a model for us on how to live the Principle and Foundation. In his Letter to the people of Philippi he writes:

> I have learned to be satisfied with what I have. I know what it is to be in need and what it is to have more than enough. I have learned this secret, so that anywhere, at any time, I am content, whether I am full or hungry, whether I have too much or too little. (Philippians 4:11-12)

He is able to be this way because of the grace of God; he has the strength to say "Yes" to all conditions because he has discovered the source of true happiness: freedom from attachment.

The ancient Chinese philosopher and poet Lao Tzu expressed it in these words:

> There is no disaster greater than not being content; there is no misfortune greater than being covetous.[7]

> When you are content to be simply yourself and don't compare or compete everybody will respect you.[8]

But oh, how we cling to that which we think defines us! A modern poet, William J. Rewak, expresses this well in his poem "Paraphernalia."

What do we get from all the connectedness
we've devised? My iPhone speaks to my iPad
which gurgles into my desktop and eventually
flashes onto my TV. What we do with wireless
we have done until now with sly looks, vocal chords,
flesh-on-flesh, even a kick in the butt; all of this,
however has been digitalized to fit a more
convenient space; it's been diagrammatically
arranged for easier access, more effective control.
Circles have become squares, cloudbursts deleted,
I sit up straight rather than slouch, have forgotten
how to preface gracefully or conclude with a coda.
What do I get? I have become a shadow, a mite;
But if you threaten my paraphernalia, I can still bite.[9]

The tenth commandment urges us to direct our affections rightly and to find consolation in what we have, rather than pining for what we don't have. This involves redefining 'success.' As the late educator Ian Knox put it: "What is our personal understanding and measurement of 'success'? Acquisition of material goods? power? influence? Or is it our improvement as loving, caring human persons?"[10]

Virtue ethics has something to say in our battle against coveting. Virtue ethics focuses on the goal of our lives. What kind of person do I wish to become? What virtues do I need to develop in order to reach my goals – of being content with what I have, of being more loving and caring? Theologian James F. Keenan poses three key questions we can ask ourselves in light of virtue ethics:

- Who am I?
- Who am I called to become?
- How do I get there?[11]

These three questions invite us to define our identity beyond material possessions; to work towards authentic self-understanding by setting goals; and to outline and undertake our journey to meet those goals.

Conclusion

Ideally, we learn the lessons of the Ten Commandments from our parents or other significant adult figures. I was fortunate. Not only were my parents people of faith, but I also went to a Catholic elementary school where the Sisters gave us a strong foundation for our beliefs, which of course included learning the commandments.

In this chapter we have considered two vices – envy and greed – and the need to have a 'poverty of spirit', which manifests itself in a healthy detachment from material goods in order to combat covetousness. The following two stories address greed and the attitude of positive detachment.

Dr. Steve Thomas is the son of the legendary Las Vegas banker E. Parry Thomas. E. Parry Thomas and his best friend, Jerry Mack, saw the potential of Las Vegas early on and were instrumental in helping to build the city. Dr. Steve relates a story in which he learned a valuable business lesson against greed.

> I remember one time coming to Dad and asking him about a business deal I was offered that sounded really good to me. What I got from his answer was he thought I was getting a better deal than the person who was offering it to me. He said, 'That sounds really great for you, but if it isn't as good for the guy you are doing business with then it's not going to last. It's not a good business deal unless you both end up better off.[12]

He explains:

> Dad taught us through his example mostly that wealth of any kind, or resources of any kind, are a responsibility as much as a blessing. You're responsible for what you have and how you use it. There's a stewardship in a way.[13]

The second story involves a friend of mine, Dominic Marrocco, and me. Like E. Parry Thomas, Dominic is a wealthy businessman with a strong commitment to philanthropy. Dominic wanted to start what is known as a Benefit Corporation: a corporate form available in certain American states, designed for 'for-profit' entities that wish to consider society and the environment in addition to profit in their decision-making process.[14] Dominic told me about this venture one day over lunch. He wanted me to be on the board of the corporation and partake in some of the profits. I explained to him that because I have made a vow of poverty, I would not be able to be on the board, but I would be happy to be a kind of spiritual counsel to it and the members.

The split of the profits was to be 15% to the three board members, 30% to Dominic's brother, who would manage the corporation, and 55% to Dominic. The following day, Dominic and I met with the other people involved in the project. This was to be a lesson for me of someone in business with true generosity of heart and positive detachment. After Dominic explained his proposal to the prospective board members, he said, "Here is how we will divide the profits: 15% will be divided among the three board members, 30% will go to my brother, and 55% will go to me – but I am giving my 55% to Fr. Max." I was pleasantly surprised at this new development and a bit bemused, as in his good-heartedness he had one-upped me on being detached!

I can think of no better way to end this chapter and the book than to quote from St. Paul in his letter to the Romans:

> Owe no debt to anyone except the debt that binds us to love one another. The one who loves his neighbour has fulfilled the law. The commandments,'You shall not commit adultery; you shall not murder; you shall not steal; you shall not covet,' and any other commandment there may be are all summed up in this: 'You shall love your neighbour as yourself.'(13:8-9)

A Closing Prayer

God, strength of those who hope in You,
graciously give me poverty of spirit
so that the intentions of my heart
are directed to You and Your values.
Free me of any greed I may have –
a distortion of the heart –
that I may be content with what I have.
Keep me from comparing myself to others
that I may be grateful for what Your Providence
has given to me.
Direct my affections rightly that no envy touch my soul.
Grant me always the help of Your Grace
that I may follow Your commandments and
by my deeds help to further
Your Kingdom.
Amen.

Notes

Introduction

1   Ian Knox, *Theology for Teachers*, 3rd ed. (Toronto: Novalis, 1999), 261–73.

2   Abraham Joshua Heschel, *The Sabbath* (New York: Farrar Straus Giroux, 2005), p. 13.

3   *Magnificat*, Vol. 15, No. 13 (March 2014), 376.

4   Ibid., 377.

5   Richard T. De George, "The History of Business Ethics," in *The Accountable Corporation*, Vol. 2, Marc J. Epstein and Kirk O. Hanson, eds. (Westport, CT: Praeger Publishers, 2006), 47–48. Professor De George is also the Director of the International Center for Ethics in Business at the University of Kansas.

6   Andre L. Delbecq, Sarita Tamayo-Moraga, Bo Tep, Len Tischler and Juan Velasco, "*Ignatius and the Buddha in Conversation*," 2014. Reprints available from Andre L. Delbecq at adelbecq@scu.edu. About the Ten Great Precepts, Zen Master Reb Anderson writes: "Even though they read like prohibitions, the Ten Great Precepts are … meant to awaken us from delusion…. Their purpose is not to control or limit living beings in any way, but to encourage the fullest flowering of life." (*Being Upright: Zen Meditation and the Bodhisattva Precepts* [Berkeley, CA: Rodmell Press, 83–84]).

7   Unless otherwise noted, scripture references are drawn from the New American Bible and the Good News Bible.

Chapter 1

1   Francis Thompson, *The Hound of Heaven* (Wilton, CT: Morehouse-Barlow, 1980), 26.

2   David L. Fleming, S.J., *The Spiritual Exercises of St. Ignatius: A Literal Translation and Contemporary Reading* (St. Louis, MO: The Institute of Jesuit Resources, 1978), 23.

3   Ibid.

4   Charles de Foucauld, in *Writings Selected*, with an introduction by Robert Ellsberg (Maryknoll, NY: Orbis Books, 1996, 1999), 92.

5   See my book *God of Many Loves* (Notre Dame, IN: Ave Maria Press, 2001), Chapter 6, "A Pilgrimage to Deeper Healing," for an in-depth account of my facing this fear and overcoming it.

6   Thomas Flowers, *God's Invitation: Meditations on a Covenant Relationship* (Mahwah, NJ: Paulist Press, 2011), 103–04. Used with permission of the publisher.

7   M. Basilea Schlink, *Mount Carmel and the Prophet Elijah* (Darmstadt-Eberstadt, West Germany: Evangelical Sisterhood of Mary, 1988), 11. (This is a pamphlet.)

Chapter 2

1   Ian Knox, C.S.Sp., *Theology for Teachers*, 3rd ed. (Toronto: Novalis, 1999), 261–62.

2   John L. McKenzie, S.J., *Dictionary of the Bible* (New York: Macmillan, 1965), 603.

3   *Catechism of the Catholic Church* (New York: Doubleday Dell, 1995), no. 2143. Further references to the Catechism will appear in the body of the text.

4   McKenzie, *Dictionary of the Bible*, 603–04.

5   See my book *God of Many Loves* (Notre Dame, IN: Ave Maria Press, 2001), Introduction.

6   Henry "Hank" Shea is now a Fellow at the University of St. Thomas School of Law and its Thomas E. Holloran Center for Ethical Leadership in the Professions, in Minnesota, and University Associate at the University of Arizona College of Law, in Tucson.

7   Hank Shea, "Top Ten List of Lessons Learned from White-Collar Criminals." http://www.stthomas.edu/news/top-10-list-lessons-learned-from-whitecollar-criminals.

8   Patrick J. Twohy, S.J., *Finding a Way Home: Indian and Catholic Spiritual Paths of the Plateau Tribes* (Spokane, WA: University Press, 1983), 272.

9   Ibid.

10 Revised English version of the *Roman Missal* (Ottawa: CCCB Publications, 2011).

11 www.theshadetree.org

12 Tracy Tomiak, *Thriving, Not Just Surviving: Living Abundantly with Pain* (AGAPE Publications, 2004), 17. Available on her website: www.hopefocused.com.

13 Ibid., 37–38. See also her "Ten Tips for Pain Management," 107–39.

14 Pope Benedict XVI, *Jesus of Nazareth: The Infancy Narratives* (New York: Image Books, 2012), 12.

Chapter 3

1   John L. McKenzie, S.J., *Dictionary of the Bible* (New York: MacMillan, 1965), 751.

2   Thomas D. Stegman, S.J., "Run that You May Obtain the Prize: Using St. Paul as a Resource for the Spiritual Exercises," *Studies in the Spirituality of Jesuits* (Winter 2012), 4. This journal is available from The Institute of Jesuit Sources, The Seminar on Jesuit Spirituality, 3601 Lindell Blvd., St. Louis, Missouri 63108-3393.

3   Jurgen Moltmann, *Theology of Hope* (New York: Harper & Row, 1967). See Chapter 3, especially pages 139–48, for his treatment of the gospel and promise.

4   From "Christian Believing," a report by the Doctrine Commission of the Church of England (London: SPCK, 1986).

5   Patrick J. Twohy, S.J., *Finding a Way Home: Indian and Catholic Spiritual Paths of the Plateau Tribes* (Spokane, WA: University Press, 1983), 119.

6   Pope John Paul II, *Ecclesia de Eucharistia* ("The Church and the Eucharist") (Sherbrooke, QC: Mediaspaul, 2003), no. 13.

7   Rev. Lawrence E. Mick, "Finding Jesus in the Eucharist: Four Ways He is Present," in *Catholic Update*, July 2005 (Cincinnati, OH: St. Anthony Messenger Press).

8   *Ecclesia de Eucharistia*, nos. 11 and 15.

9   Alice Walker, *In Search of Our Mothers' Gardens: Womanist Prose* (City: Mariner Books, 2003).

10 Abd-Ru-Shin (Oskar Ernst Bernhardt), *The Ten Commandments of God* (Gambier, OH: Grail Foundation Press, 1996.). 24,

11 See my website: www.ethicsinthemarketplace.com.

12 CFA Institute, "Want to Fix the Financial World? Start Here," 2012. Visit cfainstitute. org/StartHere to learn about the CFA Institute Integrity List.

13 www.spck.org.uk/classic-prayers/st-theresa-of-avila/

Chapter 4

1   Barbara Bate, "The Family of God, Broken and Blessed" (Bronx, NY: The Living Pulpit, July–Sept. 1999), 16.

2   Christine A. Adams, "Forgiving Your Parents for Not Being Perfect" (St. Meinrad, IN: CareNotes, #50-21243-1).

3   Bill Moyers and Robert Bly, "A Gathering of Men" (Public Affairs Television, 1990).

4   Alan D. Wolfelt, "Gender Roles and Grief: Why Men's Grief Is Naturally Complicated," *Thanatos*, Vol. 15, No. 3 (Fall 1990), 21.

5   Max Oliva, S.J., *The Masculine Spirit: Resources for Reflective Living* (Notre Dame, IN: Ave Maria Press, 1997). Available from Amazon.ca or Amazon.com.

6   John R. Boatright, *Ethics and the Conduct of Business*, 6th ed. (Upper Saddle River, NJ: Prentice Hall), 19.

7   Ibid., 93.

8   J.-Robert Ouimet, *Spirituality in Management Reconciles Human Well-Being – Productivity – Profits*, 3. Available from 300 Leo-Pariseau, bureau 2120, Montreal, QC H2X 4B3. This is known as "The Golden Book".

9   Ibid.

10   Raymond F. Collins, *Christian Morality: Biblical Foundations* (Notre Dame, IN: University of Notre Dame Press, 1986), 57.

Chapter 5

1   Jeffrey Pfeffer, "Lay off the Layoffs: Why Downsizing Is Bad for Business," *Newsweek* (February 15, 2010), 32–37.

2   COBRA was passed by United States Congress in 1985 as a means for individuals to continue health insurance coverage for a period of time after losing group coverage due to termination of employment.

3   Pope John Paul II, *Evangelium Vitae – The Encyclical Letter on Abortion, Euthanasia, and the Death Penalty in Today's World* (New York: Times Books, Random House, 1995), 188. Available at www.vatican.va. It is no. 105.

4   *United States Catholic Catechism for Adults* (Washington, D.C.: USCCB Publishing, 2006), 389–90.

5   Richard M. Gula, S.S., *Reason Informed by Faith: Foundations of Catholic Morality* (Mahwah, NJ: Paulist Press, 1989), 16–17.

6   Manuel G. Velasquez, *Business Ethics: Concepts and Cases* (Upper Saddle River, NJ: Pearson Prentice Hall, 2006), 20.

7   Tom Morris, *Philosophy for Dummies* (Foster City, CA: IDG Books Worldwide, 1999), 47.

8   Pope John Paul II, *The Gospel of Life*, no. 96.

9   *The Documents of Vatican II: Pastoral Constitution on the Church in the Modern World (Gaudium et Spes)*, No. 16 (New York: America Press, 1966), 213–14.

10   *United States Catholic Catechism for Adults*, 390.

11   Stephen L. Carter, *Integrity* (New York: Harper Perennial, 1997), 11.

12   *Seasonal Missalette: Worship Resource: April 7 to August 3, 2013* (Franklin Park, IL: World Library Publications), 316.

Chapter 6

1   James F. Keenan, S.J., *Moral Wisdom: Lessons and Texts from the Catholic Tradition* (Lanham, MD: Rowman & Littlefield, 2004), 113.

2   Ibid., 113–14.

3   Abd-ru-shin, *The Ten Commandments of God / The Lord's Prayer* (Gambier, OH: Grail Foundation Press, 1996), 36.

4   Ibid., 38.

5   *Pedro Arrupe: Essential Writings*, selected by Kevin Burke, S.J. (Maryknoll, NY: Orbis Books, 2004), 8.

6   *United States Catholic Catechism for Adults* (Washington, D.C.: USCCB Publishing, 2006), 405.

7   www.imagodeicounseling.com. Also see "Resources" on their website and then click on "Internet Sex Screening Test." This inventory asks important questions about online and offline sexual behaviour.

8   For further information on the Polaris Project, call 1-888-373-7888.

Chapter 7

1   Marianne M. Jennings, J.D., *The Seven Signs of Ethical Collapse* (New York: St. Martin's Press, 2006), 217–18.

2   Private conversation with Kirk O. Hanson on the subject of cheating.

3   The *Catechism of the Catholic Church* states: "Games of chance (card games, etc.) or wagers are not in themselves contrary to justice. They become morally unacceptable when they deprive someone of what is necessary to provide for his/her needs and those of others. The passion for gambling risks becoming an enslavement" (no. 2413).

4   *Pastoral Constitution on the Church in the Modern World*, in *The Documents of Vatican II*, no. 26 (New York: America Press, 1966).

5   Max Oliva, S.J., *Beatitudes for the Workplace* (Toronto: Novalis, 2009), 17–18. Available in the US from Twenty-Third Publications. Scarboro Missions has produced various resources using the Golden Rule; see their website: http://www.scarboromissions.ca/Golden_rule.

6   Pope Francis, *The Joy of the Gospel*: An Apostolic Exhortation (Ottawa: CCCB and Washington: USCCB, 2013), no. 58.

7   Ibid., no. 57.

8   Oliva, *Beatitudes for the Workplace*, 98ff.

9   Pope Francis, *The Joy of the Gospel*, no. 278–279.

Chapter 8

1   *Great Thoughts Treasury*: http://www.greatthoughtstreasury.com.

2   Declaration on Religious Freedom, in *The Documents of Vatican II* (*Dignitatis Humanae*), (New York: America Press, 1966), 679, no. 2.

3   *United States Catholic Catechism for Adults* (Washington, DC: United States Conference of Catholic Bishops, 2006), 432. See also *Catechism of the Catholic Church*, no. 2477.

4   In *Living with Christ*, July 2012 (New London, CT: Bayard Inc.).

5   See stopbullying.gov.

6   I draw my reflections on the true self and the false self from two sources: Thomas Merton, *New Seeds of Contemplation* (New York: New Directions, 1961) and James Finley, *Merton's Palace of Nowhere: A Search for God Through Awareness of the True Self* (Notre Dame, IN: Ave Maria Press, 1978).

7   For a fuller account of my experience in South Africa, read my article "Facing Our Fears in the Call to Act Justly," available online either under my name or by the title of the article with my name.

8   Stephen L. Carter, *Integrity* (New York: Perseus Books Group, 1996), 70. This is an excellent treatment of the virtue of integrity.

9   Ian Knox, *Theology for Teachers*, 3rd ed. (Toronto: Novalis, 1999), 269.

10 See also St. Paul's Letter to the Romans 13:8-10, on love as the fulfillment of the law.

Chapter 9

1   Hank Shea, "Top Ten List of Lessons Learned from White Collar Criminals." This is Lesson No. 3. Hank Shea is Senior Distinguished Fellow, School of Law, at the Holloran Center for Ethical Leadership in the Professions, University of St. Thomas, St. Paul, Minnesota (www.stthomas.edu/ethicalleadership).

2   Ambrose of Milan, sermon on Kings 21, in *The Living Pulpit*, Vol. 6, No. 3 (July–Sept. 1997), 35. The theme of this issue is "Money."

3   Opportunity Village is a not-for-profit organization that serves people in the southern Nevada community with intellectual disabilities.

4   Jeannie Hamrick is the Director of Educational Services for the Fundraising Research Group in Las Vegas, Nevada.

5   Andre L. Delbecq, Sarita Tamayo-Moraga, Bo Tep, Len Tischler and Juan Velasco, *Ignatius and the Buddha in Conversation*, 6. Requests for a copy of this excellent manuscript can be obtained from Andre L. Delbecq, The Institute for Spirituality of Organizational Leadership, Leavey School of Business, Santa Clara University, 500 El Camino Real, Santa Clara, CA 95053; e-mail: adelbecq@scu.edu.

6   David L. Fleming, S.J., *The Spiritual Exercises of St. Ignatius: A Literal Translation and Contemporary Reading* (St. Louis, MO: The Institute of Jesuit Sources, 1978), 23.

7   Lao Tzu, *Tao Te Ching*, D.C. Lau, trans. (Hong Kong: The Chinese University Press, 1996), XLVI, 105.

8   Lao Tzu, *Tao Te Ching*, Stephen Mitchell, trans. (HarperCollins, 1998), 8.

9   William J. Rewak, *The Orphan Bear* (North Charleston, SC: CreateSpace Independent Publishing Platform, 2014), 4. Used with permission of the author.

10 Ian Knox, *Theology for Teachers* (Toronto: Novalis, 1999), 272.

11 James F. Keenan, S.J., *Moral Wisdom: Lessons and Texts from the Catholic Tradition* (Lanham, MD: Rowman & Littlefield Publishing, 2004), 96.

12 Jack Sheehan, *Quiet Kingmaker of Las Vegas: E. Parry Thomas* (Las Vegas, NV: Stephens Press, 2009), 284–85.

13 Ibid., 259.

14 This and further information on Benefit Corporations is available from Wikipedia.